TOXOPHILUS
THE SCHOOL OF SHOOTING

(HISTORY OF ARCHERY SERIES)

BY

ROGER ASCHAM

British Library Cataloguing-in-Publication Data
A catalogue record for this book is available from the
British Library

CONTENTS

Roger Ascham

Roger Ascham was born in 1515, at Kirby Wiske, Yorkshire, England. He was a scholar and didactic writer, famous for his promotion of the vernacular and his theories on education. He was a life-long servant to royalty, serving as Princess Elizabeth's tutor in Greek and Latin between 1548 and 1550, also working in the administrations of Edward VI, Mary I, and Elizabeth I. Ascham came from a reasonably well connected family, his father, John, was steward to Baron Scrope of Bolton and he ensured that his son was well educated. Ascham spent his early education under a private tutor in the home of the famous barrister and Speaker of the House of Commons, Sir Humphrey Wingfield. At the age of fifteen, Ascham was sent to St. John's College, Cambridge, where he studied Greek, and graduated in 1534. Due to the friendship of Nicholas Metcalfe, the master of the college, Ascham was elected to a fellowship and took his M.A. degree in 1537. During his time at Cambridge, Ascham endeavoured to teach as many young scholars as he could, and one of his pupils during this period was William Grindal, who in 1544 became tutor to Princess Elizabeth. On Grindal's death, Ascham was elected as the Princess's tutor and praised her 'beauty, stature, wisdom and industry', noting that she spoke French and Italian as well as English, and wrote Greek and Latin beautifully. Ascham later served as *Latin Secretary* to Edward VI, and afterwards, Queen Mary and Elizabeth I – a difficult feat during the turbulent Tudor period. Aside from this royal employment, Ascham was an influential writer, composing *Toxophilus,* the first book on Archery in English, in 1545. Several years later, Ascham began work on *The Scholemaster,* a treatise on 'the right order of teaching', posthumously published in 1570. It was intended as an aid to private tutors, who would have mostly taught Latin in gentlemen and noblemen's houses. The 'perfect method' recommended was a double translation of Sturmius' *Select Letters of Cicero,* a method in fact taken from Cicero itself, along with a plea for gentleness and persuasion instead of coercion by beating. Ascham's personal letters were collected and published in 1576, and the *Scholemaster* was reprinted in 1571 and 1589. Ascham died before any of these works were published however. After catching a cold from working through the night on a New Year's poem to the Queen, he passed away on 30 December, 1568.

CHRONICLE

(by Edward Arber)

of

some of the principal events

in the

LIFE, WORKS, AND TIMES

OF

ROGER ASCHAM,

Fellow of St. John's College, Cambridge. Author. Tutor to Princess, afterwards Queen Elizabeth. Secretary of Embassy under Edward VI. Latin Secretary to Queens Mary and Elizabeth. Friend of Queen Elizabeth, etc.

* Probable or approximate dates.

THE chief contemporary authorities for the life of Ascham are his own works, particularly his Letters, and a Latin oration *De vitâ et obitu Rogeri Aschami*, written by Rev. Dr. Edward Graunt or Grant, Headmaster of Westminster School, and the 'most noted Latiniste and Grecian of his time.' This oration is affixed to the first collection of Ascham's Letters: the date of Grant's dedication to which is 16 February 1576.

The figures in brackets, as (40), in the present work, refer to Ascham's letters as arranged in Dr. Giles' edition.[1]

1509. April 22. Henry VIII succeeds to the throne.

1511-12.   3 Hen. VIII c. 3 required—under penalty on default of 12d[2] per month—all subjects under 60, not lame, decrepit or maimed, or having any other lawful Impediment; the Clergy, Judges etc excepted: to use shooting in the long bow. Parents were to provide every boy from 7 to 17 years, with a bow and two arrows: after 17, he was to find himself a bow and four arrows. Every Bowyer for every Yew bow he made was to make 'at least two Bows of Wych Elm or other wood of mean price,' under penalty of Imprisonment for 8 days. Butts were to be provided in every town. Aliens were not to shoot with the long bow without licence.[3]

     3 Hen. VIII c. 13 confirms 19 Hen. VII c. 4 'against shooting in Cross-bows etc,' which enacted that no one with less than 200 marks[4] a year should use. This act increased the qualification from 200 marks to 300 marks.[4]—Statutes of the Realm iii 25 32.

ROGER ASCHAM was born in the year 1515, at Kirby Wiske, (or Kirby Wicke,) a village near North Allerton in Yorkshire, of a family above the vulgar. His father, John Ascham, was house-steward in the family of Lord Scroop, and is said to have borne an unblemished reputation for honesty and uprightness of life. Margaret, wife of John Ascham, was allied to many considerable families, but her maiden name is not known. She had three sons, Thomas, Anthony, and Roger, besides some daughters; and we learn from a letter (21) written by her son Roger, in the year 1544, that she and her husband having lived together forty-seven years, at last died on the same day and almost at the same hour.

Roger's first years were spent under his father's roof, but he was received at a very youthful age into the family of Sir Anthony Wingfield, who furnished money for his education, and placed Roger, together with his own two sons, under a tutor, whose name was R. Bond. The boy had by nature a taste for books, and showed his good taste by reading English in preference to Latin, with wonderful eagerness ...—Grant. *Condensed translation by Dr. Giles in Life: see p. 10, No. 9.*

'This communication of teaching youth, maketh me remember the right worshipful, and my singular good master, Sir Humphrey Wingfield, to whom, next God, I ought to refer, for his manifold benefits bestowed on me, the poor talent of learning which God hath lent me; and for his sake do I owe my service to all other of the name and noble house of the Wingfields, both in word and deed. This worshipful man hath ever loved and used to have many children brought up in learning in his house, amongst whom I myself was one. For whom at term-times he would bring down from London both bow and shafts; and, when they should play, he would go with them himself into the field, and see them shoot; and he that shot fairest, should have the best bow and shafts; and he that shot ill-favourably, should be mocked of his fellows, till he shot better.'—*p. 135.*

In or about the year 1530, Mr. Bond ... resigned the charge of young Roger, who was now about fifteen years old, and, by the advice and pecuniary aid of his kind patron Sir Anthony, he was enabled to enter St. John's College, Cambridge, at that time the most famous seminary of learning in all England. His tutor was Hugh Fitzherbert, fellow of St. John's, whose intimate friend, George Pember, took the most lively interest in the young student. George Day—afterwards Bishop of Chichester, Sir John Cheke, Sir Thomas Smith, Dr. Redman—one of the compilers of the Book of Common Prayer, Nicholas Ridley the Martyr, T. Watson Bishop of Lincoln, Pilkington[5] Bishop of Durham, Walter Haddon, John Christopherson, Thomas Wilson, John Seton, and many others, were the distinguished contemporaries of Ascham at Cambridge.—*Grant and Giles, idem.*

He takes his B.A. 'Being a boy, new Batchelor of Art, I chanced amongst my companions to speak against the Pope: which matter was then in every man's mouth, because *Dr. Haines* and *Dr. Skippe* were come from the Court, to debate the same matter, by preaching and disputation in the university. This happened the same time, when I stood to be fellow there: my talk came to *Dr. Medcalfes* [Master of St. John's College] ere; I was called before him and the Seniors; and after grievous rebuke, and some punishment, open warning was given to all the fellows, none to be so hardy to give me his voice at that election. And yet for all those open threats, the good father himself privily procured, that I should even then be chosen fellow. But, the election being done, he made countenance of great discontentation thereat. This good man's goodness, and fatherly discretion, used towards me that one day, shall never out of my remembrance all the days of my life. And for the same cause, have I put it here, in this small record of learning. For next God's providence, surely that day, was by that good Father's means. *Dies natalis,* to me, for the whole foundation

1530 Aged 15 years.

1534 Feb. 18. Aged 18 years.

Mar. 23.

'My sweet time spent at Cambridge.' *The scholemaster, fol. 60, Ed. 1570* of the poor learning I have, and of all the furtherance, that hitherto elsewhere I have obtained.'—*Scho. fol. 55.*

1537-40.
'Before the King's Majesty established his lecture at Cambridge, I was appointed by the votes of all the university, and was paid a handsome salary, to profess the Greek tongue in public; and I have ever since read a lecture in St. John's College, of which I am a fellow.' (22) *To Sir W. Paget in 1544.*

1537 July 3
Aged 21 years.
[*die martis post festum Diui Petri et Pauli* (June 29) *Grant*]. Is installed M.A.

1538 Spring
Aged 22 years.
Visits his parents in Yorkshire, whom he has not seen for seven years.

Autumn
Date of his earliest extant letter.

1540-2.
Is at home in Yorkshire, for nearly two years, with quartan fever[6]. Probably about this time he attended the archery meetings at York and Norwich. *pp. 156, 157.*

1540 Aged 24 years.
'In the great snow,' journeying 'in the high way betwixt Topcliffe-upon-Swale;'[7] and Boroughbridge,'[7] he watches the nature of the wind by the snow-drifts. *p. 154.*

1541 Aged 25 years.
Upon his repeated application, Edward Lee, Archbishop of York, grants him a pension of 40s[8] payable at the feast of Annunciation[9] and on Michaelmas day.[9] *See* (24). This pension ceased on the death of the Archbishop in 1544.

1541-2.
33 Hen. VIII c. 9 'An Act for Maintenance of Artillery and debarring of unlawful Games.' confirms 3 Hen. VIII c. 3[3] and, *inter alia*, direct that no Bowyer shall sell a Yew bow to any between 8 and 14 years, above the price of 12d,[2] but shall have for such, Yew bows from 6d[2] to 12d:[2] and likewise shall sell bows at reasonable prices to youth from 14 to 21 years. Yew bows 'of the tax called Elke' were not to be sold above 3s 4d,[10] under penalty of 20s.[8]—*Statutes of the Realm iii 837.*

1544 *Spring Aged 28 years Ascham writes *Toxophilus.*

After Lady Day.[9]
Both his parents die. 'How hard is my lot! I first lost my brother, such an one as not only our family, but all England could hardly match, and now to lose both my parents as if I was not already overwhelmed with sorrow!' (21) *To Checke.*

Before July.
'I have also written and dedicated to the

'My sweet time spent at Cambridge.' The scholemaster, Fol. 60. Ed. 1570

7

King's Majesty a book, which is now in the press, *On the art of Shooting*, and in which I have shown how well it is fitted for Englishmen both at home and abroad, and how certain rules of art may be laid down to ensure its being learnt thoroughly by all our fellow-countrymen. This book, I hope, will be published before the King's departure, and will be no doubtful sign of my love to my country, or mean memorial of my humble learning. (22) *To Sir W. Paget.*

July–Sept. 30. The King out of the kingdom, at the head of 30,000 men at the siege of Boulogne, in France.

1545 Aged 29 years. Ascham presents *Toxophilus* to the King, in the gallery at Greenwich. He is granted a pension of £10.

He is ill again, and unable to reside at Cambridge.

1546 Aged 30 years. Succeeds Cheke as Public Orator of his University, in which capacity he conducts its correspondence.

1547. Jan. 28. Edward VI comes to the throne.

Ascham's pension which ceased on the death of Henry VIII, was confirmed and augmented by Edward VI, whom he taught to write. [Ascham's pension is one of the prominent things in his life.]

1548 Feb. Aged 32 years. Is Tutor to Princess Elizabeth, at Cheston.

1549 Sept. Aged 33 years. Attacked by her steward, he returns to the university.

1550 Aged 34 years. While at home in the country, Ascham is appointed, at the instigation of Cheke, as Secretary to Sir Richard Morison, sent out as Ambassador to Emperor Charles V.

On his way to town, has his famous interview with Lady Jane Grey at Broadgate. *Scholemaster fol. 12.*

Sept. 21. The Embassy embarks at Billingsgate, and finally reaches Augsburg on October 28: where it appears to have remained more than a year.

1552 Oct. Ascham writes, probably from Spires, *A Report and Discourse written by Roger Ascham, of the affairs and state of Germany and the*

8

Emperor Charles his court, during certain years while the said Roger was there. Published at London, the next year, without date.

1553. July 6. Mary succeeds to the crown.

1553 July 7.	Writes from Brussels.
	On the death of the King the Embassy is recalled.
1554 April.	Through a Protestant, Ascham escapes persecution; his pension is renewed and increased.
May 7.	He is made Latin Secretary to the Queen, with a salary of 40 marks.[a]
	Resigns his Fellowship and Office of Public Orator.
June 1. Aged 38 years.	Marries Margaret Howe.
	He sometimes reads Greek with Princess Elizabeth.

1558. November 17. Elizabeth begins to reign.

	Ascham's pension and Secretaryship are continued.
1560 Mar. 11 Aged 44 years.	Is made prebend of Wetwang[11], in York Cathedral. He had now possession of a considerable income. It would be satisfactory if he could be cleared from the suspicion of a too great love for cock-fighting.
1563 Dec. 10 Aged 47 years.	The Court being at Windsor on account of the plague in London, Sir W. Cecil gave a dinner in his chamber. A conversation on Education arose on the news 'that diverse Scholars of Eton be run away from the School, for fear of beating.' Sir Richard Sackville, then silent, afterwards renewed the subject with Ascham; who finally writes for his grandson, Robert Sackville, *The Scholemaster*, first published by his widow in 1570.

His constitution has been enfeebled by frequent attacks of ague. Imprudently sitting up late to finish some Latin verses which he designed to present to the Queen as a new-year's gift, and certain letters to his friends, he contracted a dangerous malady, during which he was visited and consoled by his pious friend Alexander Nowell, Dean of St. Paul's, and William Gravet, a Prebendary of that church and Vicar of St. Sepulchre's, Lon-

9

Illness and death

1568 Dec. 30
Aged 53 years.
1569 Jan. 4.

don. Ascham died 30 December 1568. His last words were 'I desire to depart and to be with Christ.'

He was buried in Sepulchre's.[12] Nowell preached his funeral sermon, and testified that he never saw or heard of a person of greater integrity of life, or who was blessed with a more christian death. Queen Elizabeth, when informed of his decease, declared that she would rather have lost £10,000 than her tutor Ascham.

Buchanan did honour to his memory in the following epitaph:

Aschamum extinctutn patriœ, Graiœque Camœnœ,

Et Latiœ verâ cum pietate dolent.

Principibus vixit carus, jucundis amicis,

Re modicâ, in mores dicere fama nequit.

which has been thus rendered by Archdeacon Wrangham:

O'er Ascham, withering in his narrow urn,
The   muses—English,
Grecian,   Roman—mourn:
Though poor, to greatness dear, to friendship just:
No scandal's self can taint his hallow'd dust.

Cooper. Ath. Cantag. p. 266

NOTES

1. Dr. Giles' edition 1864–5.
2. 12d = one shilling = 5 pence (5p), 6d = 3 pence (3p).
3. 3 Hen. VIII c. 3 was repealed by the Statute Law Revision Act c. 125, 1863.
4. One mark = 13s 4d = 67p, 40 marks = £2613s 4d = £26 67P. 200 marks = £133 6s 8d=£133 33p, 300 marks = £200 os od = £200 op.
5. James Pilkington was Master of St. John's College, Cambridge from 1559 to 1561 before he was the Bishop of Durham.
6. Quartan fever is an ague or acute fever which occurs every fourth day.
7. Topcliffe-upon-Swale and Boroughbridge are villages in the north-west of Yorkshire.
8. 40s = £2, 20s = £1.
9. The feast of Annunciation (Lady Day) is on March 25th, and Michaelmas day is on September 29th.
10. 3S 4d = 17p.
11. Wetwang is a village in the east of Yorkshire.
12. St. Sepulchre's in Holborn, London.

DEDICATION

———

To the most gracious, and our most dread Sovereign Lord, King Henry the VIIL., by the Grace of God, King of England, France, and Ireland, Defender of the Faith, and of the Church of England, and also of Ireland, in earth Supreme Head, next under Christ, be all Health, Victory, and Felicity.

What time as, most Gracious Prince, your Highness, this last year past, took that your most honourable and victorious journey into France, accompanied with such a port of the Nobility and Yeomanry of England, as neither hath been like known by experience, nor yet read of in history: accompanied also with the daily prayers, good hearts, and wills, of all and every one your Grace's subjects left behind you here at home in England; the same time, I being at my book in Cambridge, sorry that my little ability could stretch out no better to help forward so noble an enterprise, yet with my good will, prayer, and heart, nothing behind him that was foremost of all, conceived a wonderful desire, by the prayer, wishing, talking, and communication, that was in every man's mouth, for your Grace's most victorious return, to offer up something, at your home-coming, to your Highness, which should both be a token of my love and duty toward your Majesty, and also a sign of my good mind and zeal toward my country.

This occasion, given to me at that time, caused me to take in hand again this little purpose of shooting, begun of me before, yet not ended then, for other studies more meet for that trade of living, which God and my friends had set me unto. But when your Grace's most joyful and happy victory prevented my daily and speedy diligence to perform this matter, I was compelled to wait another time, to prepare and offer up this little book unto your Majesty. And when it hath pleased your Highness, of your infinite goodness, and also your most honourable Council, to know and peruse over the contents, and some part of this book, and so to allow it, that other men might read it, through the furtherance and setting forth of the right worshipful and my singular good master, Sir William Paget, Knight, most worthy secretary to your Highness, and most open and ready succour to all poor honest learned men's suits, I most humbly beseech your Grace to take in good worth this little treatise, purposed, begun, and ended of me only for this intent, that labour, honest pastime, and virtue, might recover again that place and right, that idleness, unthrift, gaming, and vice, have put them fro [from].

And although to have written this book either in Latin

or Greek (which thing I would be very glad yet to do, if I might surely know your Grace's pleasure therein), had been more easy and fit for my trade in study; yet nevertheless, I, supposing it no point of honesty, that my commodity should stop and hinder any part either of the pleasure or profit of many, have written this English matter, in the English tongue, for Englishmen; where in this I trust that your Grace (if it shall please your Highness to read it) shall perceive it to be a thing honest for me to write, pleasant for some to read, and profitable for many to follow; containing a pastime honest for the mind, wholesome for the body, fit for every man, vile for no man, using the day and open place for honesty to rule it : not lurking in corners for misorder to abuse it. Therefore I trust it shall appear to be both a sure token of my zeal to set forward shooting, and some sign of my mind towards honesty and learning.

Thus will I trouble your Grace no longer, but with my daily prayer I will beseech God to preserve your Grace in all health and felicity: to the fear and overthrow of all your enemies: to the pleasure, joyfulness, and succour of all your Subjects: to the utter destruction of Papistry and Heresy: to the continual setting forth of God's word and his glory.

Your Grace's most bounden Scholar,

ROGER ASCHAM.

TO ALL
GENTLEMEN AND YEOMEN
OF ENGLAND

———————

Bias the wise man came to Croesus the rich King, on a time when he was making new ships, purposing to have subdued by water the out isles lying betwixt Greece and Asia Minor. "What news now in Greece?" said the King to Bias. "None other news but these," saith Bias: "that the isles of Greece have prepared a wonderful company of horsemen to over-run Lydia withal." "There is nothing under heaven," saith the King, "that I would so soon wish, as that they durst be so bold to meet us on the land with horse." "And think you," saith Bias, "that there is any thing which they would sooner wish, than that you should be so fond to meet them on the water with ships?" And so Croesus, hearing not the true news, but perceiving the wise man's mind and counsel, both gave then over making of his ships, and left also behind him a wonderful example for all commonwealths to follow: that is, evermore to regard and set most by that thing where-unto nature hath made them most apt, and use hath made them most fit.

By this matter I mean the shooting in the long bow, for Englishmen; which thing with all my heart I do wish, and if I were of authority,* I would counsel all the gentlemen and yeomen of England, not to change it with any other thing, how good soever it seems to be; but that still, according to the old wont of England, youth should use it for the most honest pastime in peace, that men might handle it as a most sure weapon in war. Other strong weapons,† which both experience doth prove to be good, and the wisdom of the King's Majesty and his council provides to be had, are not ordained to take away shooting; but that both, not compared together whether should be better than the other, but so joined together that the one should be always an aid and help for the other, might so strengthen the realm on all sides, that no kind of enemy, in any kind of weapon, might pass and go beyond us.

For this purpose, I, partly provoked by the counsel of some gentlemen, partly moved by the love which I have always borne toward shooting, have written this little treatise ; wherein, if I have not satisfied any man, I trust he will the rather be content with my doing, because I am (I suppose) the first, which hath said any thing in this matter, (and few beginnings be perfect, saith wise men;) and also because, if I have said amiss, I am content that any man amend it: or, if I have said too little, any man that will, to add what him pleaseth to it.

My mind is, in profiting and pleasing every man, to hurt or displease no man, intending none other purpose, but that youth might be stirred to labour, honest pastime, and virtue, and as much as lieth in me, plucked from idleness, unthrifty games, and vice: which thing I have laboured only in this book, showing how fit shooting is for all kinds of men; how honest a pastime for the mind; how wholesome an exercise for the body; not vile for great men to use, not costly for poor men to sustain, not lurking in holes and corners for ill men at their pleasure to misuse it, but abiding in the open sight and face of the world, for good men, if it fault, by their wisdom to correct it.

And here I would desire all gentlemen and yeomen to use this pastime in such a mean, that the outrageousness of great gaming should not hurt the honesty of shooting, which, of his own nature, is always joined with honesty; yet for men's faults oftentimes blamed unworthily, as all good things have been, and evermore shall be.

If any man would blame me, either for taking such a matter in hand, or else for writing it in the English tongue, this answer I may make him, that when the best of the realm think it honest for them to use, I one of the meanest sort, ought not to suppose it vile for me to write; and though to have written it in another tongue, had been both more profitable for my study, and also more honest* for my name, yet I can think my labour well bestowed, if with a little hinderance of my profit and name, may come any furtherance to the pleasure or commodity of the gentlemen and yeomen of England, for whose sake I took this matter in hand. And as for the Latin or Greek tongue, every thing is so excellently done in them, that none can do better: in the English tongue, contrary, every thing in a manner so meanly both for the matter and handling, that no man can do worse. For therein the least learned, for the most part, have been always most ready to write. And they which had least hope in Latin, have been most bold in English: when surely every man that is most ready to talk, is not most able to write. He that will write well in any tongue, must follow this counsel of Aristotle, to speak as the common people do, to think as wise men do: and so should every man understand him, and the judgment of wise men allow him. Many English writers have not done so, but using strange words, as Latin, French, and Italian, do make all things dark and hard. Once I communed with a man which reasoned the English tongue to be enriched and increased thereby, saying, "Who will not praise that feast where a man shall drink at a dinner both wine, ale, and beer?" "Truly (quoth I) they be all good, every one taken by himself alone, but if you put malmsey and sack, red wine and white, ale and beer, and all in one pot, you shall make a drink neither easy to be known, nor yet wholesome for the body." Cicero, in following Isocrates, Plato, and Demosthenes, increased the Latin tongue after another sort. This way, because divers men that write do not know, they can neither follow it, because of their ignorance, nor yet will praise it for very arrogancy, two faults, seldom the one out of the other's company.

English writers by diversity of time have taken divers matters in hand. In our fathers' time nothing was read but books of feigned chivalry, wherein a man by reading should be led to none other end, but only to manslaughter and bawdry. If any man suppose they were good enough to pass the time withal, he is deceived. For surely vain words do work no small thing in vain, ignorant, and young minds, especially if they be given any thing thereunto of their own nature. These books (as I have heard say) were made the most part in abbeys and monasteries,—a very likely and fit fruit of such an idle and blind kind of living. In our time now, when every man is given to know, much rather than to live well, very many do write, but after such a fashion as very many do shoot. Some shooters take in hand stronger bows than they be able to maintain.* This thing maketh them sometime to outshoot the mark, sometime to shoot far wide, and perchance hurt some that look on. Other that never learned to shoot, nor yet knoweth good shaft nor bow, will be as busy as the best, but such one commonly plucketh down a side,† and crafty archers which be against him, will be both glad of him, and also ever ready to lay and bet with him, it were better for such one to sit down than shoot. Other there be, which have very good bow and shafts, and good knowledge in shooting, but they have been brought up in such evil favoured shooting, that they can neither shoot[‡] fair nor yet near. If any man will apply these things together, he shall not see the one far differ from the other. And I also, amongst all other, in writing this little treatise, have followed some young shooters, which both will begin to shoot, for a little money, and also will use to shoot once or twice about the mark for nought, afore they begin a-good. And therefore did I take this little matter in hand, to assay myself, and hereafter, by the grace of God, if the judgment of wise men, that look on, think that I can do any good, I may perchance cast my shaft among other, for better game. Yet in writing this book, some men will marvel perchance, why that I, being an imperfect shooter, should take in hand to write of making a perfect archer: the same man, peradventure, will marvel how a whetstone, which is blunt, can make the edge of a knife sharp. I would the same man should consider also, that in going about any matter, there be four things to be considered, doing, saying, thinking, and perfectness: first, there is no man that doth so well, but he can say better, or else some men, which be now stark nought, should be too good: again, no man can utter with his tongue so well as he is able to imagine with his mind, and yet perfectness itself is far above all thinking: then, seeing that saying is one step nearer perfectness than doing, let every man leave marvelling why my word shall rather express, than my deed shall perform, perfect shooting.

I trust no man will be offended with this little book, except it be some fletchers* and bowyers, thinking hereby that many that love shooting shall be taught to refuse such naughty wares as they would utter. Honest fletchers and bowyers do not so, and they that be unhonest, ought rather to amend themselves for doing ill, than being angry with me for saying well. A fletcher hath even so good a quarrel to be angry with an archer that refuseth an ill shaft, as a blade-smith hath to a fletcher that forsaketh to buy of him a naughty knife: for as an archer must be content that a fletcher know a good shaft in every point for the perfecter making of it; so an honest fletcher will also be content that a shooter know a good shaft in every point, for the perfecter using of it; because the one knoweth like a fletcher how to make it, the other knoweth like an archer how to use it. And seeing the knowledge is one in them both, yet the end divers, surely that fletcher is an enemy to archers and artillery which cannot be content that an archer know a shaft as well for his use in shooting, as he himself should know a shaft for his advantage in selling. And the rather, because shafts be not made so much to be sold, but chiefly to be used. And seeing that use and occupying is the end why a shaft is made, the making, as it were, a mean for occupying, surely the knowledge in every point of a good shaft, is more to be required in a shooter than a fletcher.

Yet, as I said before, no honest fletcher will be angry with me, seeing I do not teach how to make a shaft, which belongeth only to a good fletcher, but to know and handle a shaft, which belongeth to an archer. And this little book, I trust, shall please and profit both parties; for good bows and shafts shall be better known to the commodity of all shooters, and good shooting may, perchance, be the more occupied to the profit of all bowyers and fletchers. And thus I pray God that all fletchers, getting their living truly, and all archers using shooting honestly, and all manner of men that favour artillery, may live continually in health and merriness, obeying their prince as they should, and loving God as they ought: to whom, for all things, be all honour and glory for ever. Amen

* *Authority* is here used not for *Power*, but for *Credit* or *Influence*. † Fire-arms began about this time to be made for the hand, ordnance or great guns seem to have been near a century employed in war, before hand-guns were much used. * *Honest* is here used for *honourable*. * To *maintain* is to *manage*. † To *pluck down a side*, I believe, is to shoot on one side into the ground. ‡ Neither shoot gracefully nor exactly. * *Fletcher* is an arrow maker.

TOXOPHILUS.

THE FIRST BOOK OF THE SCHOOL OF SHOOTING.

PHILOLOGUS.   TOXOPHILUS.

Phi. You study too sore, Toxophile.

Tox. I will not hurt myself over-much, I warrant you.

Phi. Take heed you do not; for we physicians say, that it is neither good for the eyes in so clear a sun, nor yet wholesome for the body so soon after meat, to look upon a man's book.

Tox. In eating and studying I will never follow any physic; for if I did I am sure I should have small pleasure in the one, and less courage in the other. But what news drave you hither, I pray you?

Phi. Small news, truly; but as I came on walking, I fortuned to come with three or four that went to shoot at the pricks; and when I saw not you amongst them, but at the last espied you looking on your book here so sadly,* I thought to come and hold you with some communication, lest your book should run away with you. For methought by your wavering pace and earnest looking, your book led you, not you it.

Tox. Indeed, as it chanced, my mind went faster than my feet, for I happened here to read in *Phædro* Platonis, a place that entreats wonderfully of the nature of souls; which place, whether it were for the passing eloquence of Plato and the Greek tongue, or for the high and godly description of the matter, kept my mind so occupied that it had no leisure to look to my feet. For I was reading how some souls, being well feathered, flew always about heaven and heavenly matters; other some, having their feathers mowted away and drooping, sank down into earthly things.

Phi. I remember the place very well, and it is wonderfully said of Plato; and now I see it was no marvel though your feet failed you, seeing your mind flew so fast.

Tox. I am glad now that you letted me, for my head aches with looking on it; and because you tell me so, I am very sorry that I was not with those good fellows you spake upon, for it is a very fair day for a man to shoot in.

Phi. And, methinks you were a great deal better occupied and in better company; for it is a very fair day for a man to go to his book in.

Tox. All days and weathers will serve for that purpose, and surely this occasion was ill lost.

Phi. Yea, but clear weather maketh clear minds; and it is best, as I suppose, to spend the best time upon the best things: and methought you shot very well, and at that mark at which every good scholar should most busily shoot at. And I suppose it be a great deal more pleasure also to see a soul fly in Plato, than a shaft fly at the pricks. I grant you, shooting is not the worst thing in the world; yet if we shoot, and time shoot, we are not like to be great winners at the length. And you know also we scholars have more earnest and weighty matters in hand; nor we be not born to pastime and play, as you know well enough who saith.

Tox. Yet the same man in the same place, Philologe, by your leave, doth admit wholesome, honest, and mannerly pastimes, to be as necessary to be mingled with sad matters of the mind, as eating and sleeping is for the health of the body, and yet we be born for neither of both. And Aristotle himself saith, that although it were a fond and a childish thing to be too earnest in pastime and play, yet doth he affirm, by the authority of the old poet Epicharmus, that a man may use play for earnest matter sake. And in another place, that, as rest is for labour, and medicines for health; so is pastime, at times, for sad and weighty study.

Phi. How much in this matter is to be given to the authority either of Aristotle or Tully, I cannot tell, seeing sad men may well enough speak merrily for a merry matter: this I am sure, which thing this fair wheat (God save it) maketh me remember, that those husbandmen which rise earliest and come latest home, and are content to have their dinner and other drinkings brought into the field to them for fear of losing of time, have fatter barns in harvest, than they which will either sleep at noon-time of the day, or else make merry with their neighbours at the ale. And so a scholar that purposeth to be a good husband, and desireth to reap and enjoy much fruit of learning, must till and sow thereafter.* Our best seed time, which be scholars, as it is very timely, and when we be young, so it endureth not over-long, and therefore it may not be let slip one hour: our ground is very hard and full of weeds, our horse wherewith we be drawn, very wild, as Plato saith. And infinite other mo lets, which will make a thrifty scholar take heed how he spendeth his time in sport and play.

Tox. That Aristotle and Tully speak earnestly, and as they thought, the earnest matter which they entreat upon doth plainly prove. And, as for your husbandry, it was more probably* told with apt words proper to the thing, than thoroughly proved with reasons belonging to our matter. For, contrariwise, I heard myself a good husband at his book once say, that to omit study some time of the day and some time of the year, made as much for the increase of learning as to let the land lie some time fallow, maketh for the better increase of corn. This we see, if the land be ploughed every year, the corn cometh thin up: the ear is short, the grain is small, and, when it is brought into the barn and threshed, giveth very evil fall.[†] So those which never leave poring on their books, have oftentimes as thin invention as other poor men have, and as small wit and weight in it as in other men's. And thus your husbandry, methinks, is more like the life of a covetous snudge that oft very evil proves, than the labour of a good husband that knoweth well what he doth. And surely the best wits to learning must needs have much recreation and ceasing from their book, or else they mar themselves; when base and dumpish wits can never be hurt with continual study, as ye see in luting that a treble minikin string must always be let dowr but at such time as when a man must needs play, when the base and dull string needeth never to be moved out of his place. The same reason I find true in two bows that I have, whereof the one is quick of cast, trick,[‡] and trim both for pleasure and profit: the other is a lug, slow of cast, following the string, more sure for to last than pleasant for to use. Now, Sir, it chanced this other night, one in my chamber would needs bend them to prove their strength, but (I cannot tell how) they were both left bent till the next day at after-dinner: and when I came to them, purposing to have gone on shooting, I found my good bow clean cast[*] on the one side, and as weak as water, that surely, if I were a rich man, I had rather have spent a crown; and as for my lug, it was not one whit the worse, but shot by and by as well and as far as ever it did. And even so I am sure that good wits, except they be let down like a treble string, and unbent like a good casting bow, they will never last and be able to continue in study. And I know where I speak this, Philologe; for I would not say thus much afore young men, for they will take some occasion to study little enough. But I say it therefore, because I know, as little study getteth little learning, or none at all, so the most study getting not the most learning of all. For a man's wit sore occupied in earnest study must be as well recreated with some honest pastime, as the body sore laboured must be refreshed with sleep and quietness, or else it cannot endure very long, as the noble poet saith:

What thing wants quiet and merry rest, endures but a small while.[†]

And I promise you shooting, by my judgment, is the most honest pastime of all, and such one, I am sure, of all other, that hindereth learning little or nothing at all, whatsoever you and some others say, which are a great deal sorer against it always than you need to be.

Phi. Hindereth learning little or nothing at all! that were a marvel to me truly; and I am sure, seeing you say so, you have some reason wherewith you can defend shooting withal; and as for will, (for the love that you bear towards shooting,) I think there shall lack none in you. Therefore, seeing we have so good leisure both, and nobody by to trouble us, and you so willing and able to defend it, and I so ready and glad to hear what may be said of it, I suppose we cannot pass the time better over, neither you for the honesty* of your shooting, nor I for mine own mind sake, than to see what can be said with it or against it; and specially in these days when so many doeth use it, and every man, in a manner, doeth commune of it.

Tox. To speak of shooting, Philologe, truly I would I were so able, either as I myself am willing, or yet as the matter deserveth ; but seeing with wishing we can not have one now worthy, which so worthy a thing can worthily praise, and although I had rather have any other to do it than myself, yet myself rather than no other, I will not fail to say in it what I can. Wherein if I say little, lay that of my little ability, not of the matter itself, which deserveth no little thing to be said of it.

Phi. If it deserve no little thing to be said of it, Toxphile, I marvel how it chanceth then that no man hitherto hath written any thing of it; wherein you must grant me, that either the matter is nought, unworthy, and barren to be written upon, or else some men are to blame which both love it and use it, and yet could never find in their heart to say one good word of it; seeing that very trifling matters hath not lacked great learned men to set them out, as gnats† and nuts, and many other mo like things; wherefore either you may honestly lay very great fault upon men, because they never yet praised it, or else I may justly take away no little thing from shooting because it never yet deserved it.

Tox. Truly, herein, Philologe, you take not so much from it as you give to it. For great and commodious things are never greatly praised, not because they be not worthy, but because their excellency needeth no man's praise, having all their commendation of them self, not borrowed of other men his lips, which rather praise themselves in speaking much of a little thing, than that matter which they entreat upon. Great and good things be not praised: "For who ever praised Hercules?" (saith the Greek proverb). And that no man hitherto hath written any book of shooting, the fault is not to be laid in the thing which was worthy to be written upon, but of men which were negligent in doing it, and this was the cause thereof, as I suppose. Men that used shooting most and knew it best, were not learned; men that were learned used little shooting, and were ignorant in the nature of the thing, and so few men hath been that hitherto were able to write upon it. Yet how long shooting hath continued, what commonwealths hath most used it, how honest a thing it is for all men, what kind of living soever they follow, what pleasure and profit cometh of it, both in peace and war, all manner of tongues and writers, Hebrew, Greek, and Latin, hath so plentifully spoken of it, as of few other things like. So what shooting is, how many kinds there is of it, what goodness is joined with it, is told; only how it is to be learned and brought to a perfectness amongst men, is not told.

Phi. Then, Toxophile, if it be so as you do say, let us go forward and examine how plentifully this is done that you speak; and, first, of the invention of it; then what honesty and profit is in the use of it, both for war and peace, more than in other pastimes; last of all, how it ought to be learned amongst men, for the increase of it. Which thing if you do, not only I now, for your communication, but many other mo, when they shall know of it, for your labour, and shooting itself also (if it could speak) for your kindness, will can you very much thank.

Tox. What good things men speak of shooting, and what good things shooting brings to men, as my wit and knowledge will serve me, gladly shall I say my mind. But how the thing is to be learned, I will surely leave to some other, which, both for greater experience in it, and also for their learning, can set it out better than I.

Phi. Well, as for that, I know both what you can do in shooting by experience, and that you can also speak well enough of shooting for your learning: but go on with the first part. And I do not doubt but what my desire, what your love toward it, the honesty of shooting, the profit that may come thereby to many other, shall get the second part out of you at the last.

Tox. Of the first finders out of shooting, divers men diversely do write. Claudian the poet saith, that nature gave example of shooting first by the porpentine,* which doth shoot his pricks, and will hit any thing that fights with it; whereby men learned afterward to imitate the same, in finding out both bow and shafts. Pliny referreth it to Scythes the son of Jupiter. Better and more noble writers bring shooting from a more noble inventor; as Plato, Callimachus, and Galen, from Apollo. Yet long afore those days do we read in the Bible of shooting expressly; and also, if we shall believe Nicholas de Lyra, Lamech killed Cain with a shaft. So this great continuance of shooting doth not a little praise shooting; nor that neither doth not a little set it out, that it is referred to the invention of Apollo, for the which point shooting is highly praised of Galen: where he saith, that mean crafts be first found out by men or beasts, as weaving by a spider, and such other; but high and commendable sciences by gods, as shooting and music by Apollo. And thus shooting, for the necessity of it, used in Adam's days, for the nobleness of it referred to Apollo, hath not been only commended in all tongues and writers, but also had in great price, both in the best commonwealths in war time for the defence of their country, and of all degrees of men in peace time, both for the honesty that is joined with it, and the profit that followeth of it.

Phi. Well, as concerning the finding out of it, little praise is gotten to shooting thereby, seeing good wits may most easily of all find out a trifling matter. But whereas you say, that most commonwealths have used it in war time, and all degrees of men may very honestly use it in peace time, I think you can neither show by authority nor yet prove by reason.

Tox. The use of it in war time I will declare hereafter. And first, how all kinds and sorts of men (what degree soever they be) have at all times afore, and now may honestly use it, the example of most noblemen very well doth prove.

Cyaxares, the King of the Medes, and great grandfather to Cyrus, kept a sort of Scythians with him only for this purpose, to teach his son Astyages to shoot. Cyrus being a child was brought up in shooting; which thing Xenophon would never have made mention on, except it had been fit for all Princes to have used: seeing that Xenophon wrote Cyrus life (as Tully saith) not to show what Cyrus did, but what all manner of Princes both in pastimes and earnest matters ought to do.

Darius, the first of that name, and King of Persia, showed plainly how fit it is for a King to love and use shooting, which commanded this sentence to be graven in his tomb for a princely memory and praise:

> Darius the King lieth buried here,
> That in shooting and riding had never peer.

Again, Domitian the Emperor was so cunning in shooting, that he could shoot betwixt a man's fingers standing afar off, and never hurt him. Commodus also was so excellent, and had so sure a hand in it, that there was nothing within his reach and shot, but he would hit it in what place he would; as beasts running, either in the head, or in the heart, and never miss; as Herodian saith he saw himself, or else he could never have believed it.

Phi. Indeed you praise shooting very well, in that you show that Domitian and Commodus love shooting; such an ungracious couple, I am sure, as a man shall not find again, if he raked all hell for them.

Tox. Well, even as I will not commend their illness, so ought not you to dispraise their goodness; and indeed, the judgment of Herodian upon Commodus is true of them both, and that was this: that beside strength of body and good shooting, they had no princely thing in them; which saying, methink, commends shooting wonderfully, calling it a princely thing. Furthermore, how commendable shooting is for Princes, Themistius, the noble philosopher, showeth in a certain oration made to Theodosius the Emperor, wherein he doth commend him for three things, that he used of a child; for shooting, for riding of a horse well, and for feats of arms.

Moreover, not only Kings and Emperors have been brought up in shooting, but also the best commonwealths that ever were, have made goodly acts and laws for it: as the Persians, which under Cyrus conquered, in a manner, all the world, had a law that their children should learn three things only from five years old unto twenty; to ride an horse well, to shoot well, to speak truth always and never lie. The Romans (as Leo the Emperor in his book of sleights of war telleth) had a law that every man should use shooting in peace time, while he was forty years old, and that every house should have a bow and forty shafts ready for all needs; the omitting of which law (saith Leo) amongst the youth, hath been the only occasion why the Romans lost a great deal of their empire. But more of this I will speak when I come to the profit of shooting in war. If I should rehearse the statutes made of noble Princes of England in Parliaments, for the setting forward of shooting through this realm, and especially that act made for shooting the third year of the reign of our most dread sovereign Lord King Henry the VIIIth, I could be very long. But these few examples, especially of so great men and noble commonwealths, shall stand in stead of many.

Phi. That such Princes and such commonwealths have much regarded shooting, you have well declared. But why shooting ought so of itself to be regarded, you have scarcely yet proved.

Tox. Examples, I grant, out of histories do show a thing to be so, not prove a thing why it should be so. Yet this I suppose, that neither great men's qualities, being commendable, be without great authority, for other men honestly to follow them; nor yet those great learned men that wrote such things lack good reason justly at all times for any other to approve them. Princes, being children, ought to be brought up in shooting, both because it is an exercise most wholesome, and also a pastime most honest; wherein labour prepareth the body to hardness, the mind to courageousness, suffering neither the one to be marred with tenderness nor yet the other to be hurt with idleness, as we read how Sardanapalus and such other were, because they were not brought up with outward honest painful pastimes to be men, but cockered up with inward, naughty, idle wantonness to be women. For how fit labour is for all youth, Jupiter or else Minos amongst them of Greece, and Lycurgus amongst the Lacedemonians, do show by their laws, which never ordained any thing for the bringing up of youth that was not joined with labour; and the labour which is in shooting of all other is best, both because it increaseth strength and preserveth health most, being not vehement but moderate, not overlaying any one part with weariness, but softly exercising every part with equalness, as the arms and breasts with drawing, the other parts with going, being not so painful for the labour as pleasant for the pastime, which exercise, by the judgment of the best physicians, is most allowable. By shooting also is the mind honestly exercised, where a man always desireth to be best (which is a word of honesty), and that by the same way that virtue itself doth, coveting to come nighest a most perfect end, or mean standing betwixt two extremes, eschewing short, or gone, or either side wide; for the which causes Aristotle himself saith, that shooting and virtue be very like. Moreover, that shooting of all other is the most honest pastime, and hath least occasion to naughtiness joined with it, two things very plainly do prove, which be, as a man would say, the tutors and overseers to shooting: day-light, and open place where every man doth come, the maintainers and keepers of shooting from all unhonest doing. If shooting fault at any time, it hides it not, it lurks not in corners and huddermother; but openly accuseth and bewrayeth itself, which is the next way to amendment, as wise men do say. And these things, I suppose, be signs not of naughtiness for any man to disallow it, but rather very plain tokens of honesty for every man to praise it. The use of shooting also in great men's children, shall greatly increase the love and use of shooting in all the residue of youth. For mean men's minds love to be like great men, as Plato and Isocrates do say. And that every body should learn to shoot when they be young, defence of the commonwealth doth require when they be old, which thing cannot be done mightily when they be men, except they learn it perfectly when they be boys. And therefore shooting of all pastimes is most fit to be used in childhood; because it is an imitation of most earnest things to be done in manhood. Wherefore shooting is fit for great men's children, both because it strengtheneth the body with wholesome labour and pleaseth the mind with honest pastime, and also encourageth all other youth earnestly to follow the same. And these reasons (as I suppose) stirred up both great men to bring up their children in shooting, and also noble commonwealths so straitly to command shooting. Therefore seeing Princes, moved by honest occasions, hath in all commonwealths used shooting, I suppose there is none other degree of men, neither low nor high, learned nor lewd, young nor old—

Phi. You shall need wade no, further in this matter, Toxophile; but if you can prove me that scholars and men given to learning may honestly use shooting, I will soon grant you that all other sorts of men may not only lawfully, but ought of duty, to use it. But I think you cannot prove but that all these examples of shooting brought from so long a time, used of so noble Princes, confirmed by so wise men's laws and judgments, are set afore temporal men only to follow them; whereby they may the better and stronglier defend the commonwealth withal; and nothing belongeth to scholars and learned men, which have another part of the commonwealth, quiet and peaceable, put to their cure and charge, whose end, as it is diverse from the other, so there is no one way that leadeth to them both,

Tox. I grant, Philologe, that scholars and laymen have divers offices and charges in the commonwealth, which requires divers bringing up in their youth, if they shall do them as they ought to do in their age. Yet as temporal men of necessity are compelled to take somewhat of learning to do their office the better withal, so scholars may the boldlier borrow somewhat of laymen's pastimes to maintain their health in study withal. And surely, of all other things, shooting is necessary for both sorts to learn. Which thing, when it hath been evermore used in England, how much good it hath done, both old men and chronicles do tell, and also our enemies can bear us record. For if it be true as I have heard say, when the King of England hath been in France, the priests at home, because they were archers, have been able to overthrow all Scotland. Again, there is another thing, which above all other doth move me, not only to love shooting, to praise shooting, to exhort all other to shooting, but also to use shooting myself; and that is our King [Henry the Eighth] his most royal purpose and will, which in all his statutes generally doth command men, and with his own mouth most gently doth exhort men, and by his great gifts and rewards greatly doth encourage men, and with his most princely example very often doth provoke all other men to the same. But here you will come in with temporal man and scholar. I tell you plainly, scholar or unscholar, yea if I were twenty scholars, I would think it were my duty, both with exhorting men to shoot, and also with shooting myself, to help to set forward that thing which the King's wisdom, and his Council, so greatly laboureth to go forward; which thing surely they do, because they know it to be in war the defence and wall of our country; in peace an exercise most wholesome for the body, a pastime most honest for the mind, and, as I am able to prove myself, of all other most fit and agreeable with learning and learned men.

Phi. If you can prove this thing so plainly, as you speak it earnestly, then will I not only think as you do, but become a shooter, and do as you do. But yet beware, I say, lest you, for the great love you bear toward shooting, blindly judge of shooting. For love, and all other too earnest affections, be not for nought painted blind. Take heed (I say) lest you prefer shooting before other pastimes, as one Balbinus, through blind affection, preferred his lover before all other women, although she were deformed with a polypus in her nose. And although shooting may be meet some time for some scholars, and so forth, yet the fittest always is to be preferred. Therefore, if you will needs grant scholars pastime and recreation of their minds, let them use (as many of them doth) music and playing on instruments, thinks most seemly for all scholars, and most regarded always of Apollo and the Muses.

Tox. Even as I cannot deny but some music is fit for learning, so I trust you cannot choose but grant that shooting is fit also, as Callimachus doth signify in this verse:

Both merry songs and good shooting delighteth Apollo.

But as concerning whether of them is most fit for learning and scholars to use, you may say what you will for your pleasure; this I am sure, that Plato and Aristotle both, in their books entreating of the commonwealth, where they show how youth should be brought up in four things, in reading, in writing, in exercise of body, and singing, do make mention of music and all kinds of it; wherein they both agree, that music used amongst the Lydians is very ill for young men which be students for virtue and learning, for a certain nice, soft, and smooth sweetness of it, which would rather entice them to naughtiness than stir them to honesty.

Another kind of music, invented by the Dorians, they both wonderfully praise, allowing it to be very fit for the study of virtue and learning, because of a manly, rough, and stout sound in it, which should encourage young stomachs to attempt manly matters. Now whether these ballads and rounds, these galiards, pavanes, and dances, so nicely fingered, so sweetly tuned, be liker the music of the Lydians or the Dorians, you that be learned judge. And whatsoever ye judge, this I am sure, that lutes, harps, all manner of pipes, barbitons, sambukes, with other instruments every one, which standeth by fine and quick fingering, be condemned of Aristotle, as not to be brought in and used among them which study for learning and virtue.

Pallas, when she had invented a pipe, cast it away; not so much, saith Aristotle, because it deformed her face, but much rather because such an instrument belonged nothing to learning. How such instruments agree with learning, the goodly agreement betwixt Apollo God of learning, and Marsyas the Satyr, defender of piping, doth well declare, where Marsyas had his skin quite pulled over his head for his labour. "Much music marreth men's manners," saith Galen, although some man will say that it doth not so, but rather recreateth and maketh quick a man's mind; yet, methink, by reason it doth as honey doth to a man's stomach, which at the first receiveth it well, but afterward it maketh it unfit to abide any good strong nourishing meat, or else any wholesome sharp and quick drink. And even so in a manner these instruments make a man's wit so soft and smooth, so tender and quaisy, that they be less able to brook strong and tough study. Wits be not sharpened, but rather dulled and made blunt, with such sweet softness, even as good edges be blunter which men whet upon soft chalk stones.

And these things to be true, not only Plato, Aristotle, and Galen prove by authority of reason, but also Herodotus and other writers show by plain and evident example; as that of Cyrus, which, after he had overcome the Lydians, and taken their king Croesus prisoner, yet after, by the means of one Pactyas, a very heady man amongst the Lydians, they rebelled against Cyrus again; then Cyrus had by and by brought them to utter destruction, if Crœsus, being in good favour with Cyrus, had not heartily desired him not to revenge Pactyas fault in shedding their blood. But if he would follow his counsel, he might bring to pass that they should never more rebel against him. And that was this, to make them wear long kirtles to the foot, like women, and that every one of them should have a harp or a lute, and learn to play and sing. Which thing if you do, saith Croesus (as he did indeed), you shall see them quickly of men made women. And thus luting and singing take away a manly stomach, which should enter and pierce deep and hard study.

Even such another story doth Nymphodorus, an old Greek historiographer, write of one Sesosbris King of Egypt, which story, because it is somewhat long, and very like in all points to the other, and also you do well enough remember it, seeing you read it so late in Sophoclis commentaries, I will now pass over. Therefore either Aristotle and Plato know not what was good and evil for learning and virtue, and the example of wise histories be vainly set afore us, or else the minstrelsy of lutes, pipes, harps, and all other that standeth by such nice, fine, minikin fingering, (such as the most part of scholars whom I know use, if they use any,) is far more fit, for the womanishness of it, to dwell in the Court among ladies, than for any great thing in it, which should help good and sad study, to abide in the University among scholars. But perhaps you know some great goodness of such music and such instruments, whereunto Plato and Aristotle his brain could never attain; and therefore I will say no more against it.

Phi. Well, Toxophile, is it not enough for you to rail upon music, except you mock me too? But, to say the truth, I never thought myself these kinds of music fit for learning; but that which I said was rather to prove you, than to defend the matter. But yet as I would have this sort of music decay among scholars, even so do I wish, from the bottom of my heart, that the laudable custom of England to teach children their plain song and prick-song, were not so decayed throughout all the realm as it is. Which thing how profitable it was for all sorts of

45

men, those knew not so well then which had it most, as they do now which lack it most. And therefore it is true that Teucer saith in Sophocles:

> * Seldom at all good things be known how good to be
> Before a man such things do miss out of his hands.

That milk is no fitter nor more natural for the bringing up of children than music is, both Galen proveth by authority, and daily use teacheth by experience. For even the little babes lacking the use of reason, are scarce so well stilled in sucking their mother's pap, as in hearing their mother sing. Again, how fit youth is made by learning to sing, for grammar and other sciences, both we daily do see, and Plutarch learnedly doth prove, and Plato wisely did allow, which received no scholar into his school that had not learned his song before. The godly use of praising God, by singing in the church, needeth not my praise, seeing it is so praised through all the scripture; therefore now I will speak nothing of it, rather than I should speak too little of it.

Beside all these commodities, truly two degrees of men, which have the highest offices under the King in all this realm, shall greatly lack the use of singing, preachers and lawyers, because they shall not, without this, be able to rule their breasts for every purpose. For where is no distinction in telling glad things and fearful things, gentleness and cruelness, softness and vehementness, and such-like matters, there can be no great persuasion. For the hearers, as Tully saith, be much affectioned as he is that speaketh. At his words be they drawn; if he stand still in one fashion, their minds stand still with him; if he thunder, they quake; if he chide, they fear; if he complain, they sorry with him; and finally, where a matter is spoken with an apt voice for every affection, the hearers, for the most part, are moved as the speaker would. But when a man is alway in one tune, like an humble bee, or else now in the top of the church, now down, that no man knoweth where to have him; or piping like a reed, or roaring like a bull, as some lawyers do, which think they do best when they cry loudest, these shall never greatly move, as I have known many well-learned have done, because their voice was not stayed afore with learning to sing. For all voices, great and small, base and shrill, weak or soft, may be holpen and brought to a good point by learning to sing.

Whether this be true or not, they that stand most in need can tell best; whereof some I have known, which, because they learned not to sing when they were boys, were fain to take pain in it when they were men. If any man should hear me, Toxophile, that would think I did but fondly to suppose that a voice were so necessary to be looked upon, I would ask him if he thought not nature a fool, for making such goodly instruments in a man for well uttering his words; or else if the two noble orators Demosthenes and Cicero were not fools, whereof the one did not only learn to sing of a man, but also was not ashamed to learn how he should utter his sounds aptly of a dog; the other setteth out no point of rhetoric so fully in all his books, as how a man should order his voice for all kind of matters.

Therefore seeing men, by speaking, differ and be better than beasts, by speaking well better than other men, and that singing is an help toward the same, as daily experience doth teach, example of wise men doth allow, authority of learned men doth approve, wherewith the foundation of youth in all good commonwealths always hath been tempered: surely, if I were one of the Parliament-house, I would not fail to put up a bill for the amendment of this thing; but because I am like to be none this year, I will speak no more of it at this time.

Tox. It were pity truly, Philologe, that the thing should be neglected; but I trust it is not as you say.

Phi. The thing is too true; for of them that come daily to the University, where one hath learned to sing, six hath not.

But now to our shooting, Toxophile, again; wherein I suppose you cannot say so much for shooting to be fit for learning, as you have spoken against music for the same. Therefore as concerning music, I can be content to grant you your mind; but as for shooting, surely I suppose that you cannot persuade me, by no means, that a man can be earnest in it, and earnest at his book too; but rather I think that a man with a bow on his back, and shafts under his girdle, is more fit to wait upon Robin Hood than upon Apollo or the Muses.

Tox. Over-earnest shooting surely I will not over-earnestly defend; for I ever thought shooting should be a waiter upon learning, not a mistress over learning. Yet this I marvel not a little at, that ye think a man with a bow on his back is more like Robin Hood's servant than Apollo's, seeing that Apollo himself, in Alcestis of Euripides, which tragedy you read openly not long ago, in a manner glorifieth, saying this verse:

> It is my wont always my bow with me
> to bear.

Therefore a learned man ought not too much to be ashamed to bear that sometime, which Apollo, God of learning, himself was not ashamed always to bear. And because ye would have a man wait upon the Muses, and not at all meddle with shooting; I marvel that you do not remember how that the nine Muses their self, as soon as they were born, were put to nurse to a lady called Euphemis, which had a son named Erotus, with whom the nine Muses, for his excellent shooting, kept evermore company withal, and used daily to shoot together in the Mount Parnassus; and at last it chanced this Erotus to die, whose death the Muses lamented greatly, and fell all upon their knees afore Jupiter their father, and, at their request, Erotus, for shooting with the Muses on earth, was made a sign, and called Sagittarius in heaven. Therefore you see that if Apollo and the Muses either were examples indeed, or only feigned of wise men to be examples of learning, honest shooting may well enough be companion with honest study.

Phi. Well, Toxophile, if you have no stronger defence of shooting than poets, I fear if your companions which love shooting heard you, they would think you made it but a trifling and fabling matter, rather than any other man that loveth not shooting could be persuaded by this reason to love it.

Tox. Even as I am not so fond but I know that these be fables, so I am sure you be not so ignorant but you know what such noble wits, as the poets had, meant by such matters, which oftentimes, under the covering of a fable, do hide and wrap in goodly precepts of philosophy, with the true judgment of things. Which to be true, specially in Homer and Euripides, Plato, Aristotle, and Galen plainly do show; when through all their works (in a manner) they determine all controversies by these two poets, and such like authorities. Therefore, if in this matter I seem to fable and nothing prove, I am content you judge so on me, seeing the same judgment shall condemn with me Plato, Aristotle, and Galen, whom in that error I am well content to follow. If these old examples prove nothing for shooting, what say you to this, that the best learned and sagest men in this realm which be now alive, both love shooting and use shooting, as the best learned bishops that be? amongst whom, Philologe, you yourself know four or five, which as in all good learning, virtue, and sageness, they give other men example what thing they should do, even so by their shooting they plainly show what honest pastime other men given to learning may honestly use. That earnest study must be recreated with honest pastime, sufficiently I have proved afore, both by reason and authority of the best learned men that ever wrote. Then seeing pastimes be leful [*lawful*], the most fittest for learning is to be sought for. A pastime, saith Aristotle, must be like a medicine. Medicines stand by contraries; therefore, the nature of studying considered, the fittest pastime shall soon appear. In study every part of the body is idle, which thing causeth gross and cold humours to gather together and vex scholars very much, the mind is altogether bent and set on work; a pastime then must be had where every part of the body must be laboured to separate and lessen such humours withal, the mind must be unbent, to gather and fetch again his quickness withal. Thus pastimes for the mind only be nothing fit for students, because the body, which is most hurt by study, should take away no profit thereat. This knew Erasmus very well, when he was here in Cambridge; which, when he had been sore at his book (as Garret our bookbinder has very oft told me), for lack of better exercise would take his horse and ride about the market-hill and come again. If a scholar should use bowls or tennis, the labour is so vehement and unequal, which is condemned of Galen; the example very ill for other men, when by so many acts they be made unlawful. Running, leaping, and quoiting be too vile for scholars, and so not fit by Aristotle's judgment: walking alone into the field hath no token of courage in it, a pastime like a simple man which is neither flesh nor fish. Therefore, if a man would have a pastime wholesome and equal for every part of the body, pleasant and full of courage for the mind, not vile and unhonest to give ill example to laymen, not kept in gardens and corners, not lurking on the night and in holes, but evermore in the face of men, either to rebuke it when it doeth ill, or else to testify on it when it doth well; let him seek chiefly of all other for shooting.

Phi. Such common pastimes as men commonly do use, I will not greatly allow to be fit for scholars, seeing they may use such exercises very well (I suppose), as Galen himself doth allow.

Tox. These exercises I remember very well, for I read them within these two days; of the which some be these: to run up and down a hill; to climb up a long pole, or a rope, and there hang awhile; to hold a man by his arms and wave with his heels, much like the pastime that boys use in the church when their master is away; to swing and totter in a bell-rope; to make a fist, and stretch out both his arms, and so stand like a rood. To go on a man's tiptoes, stretching out the one of his arms forward, the other backward, which, if he bleared out his tongue also, might be thought to dance antic very properly. To tumble over and over, to top over tail; to set back to back, and see who can heave another's heels highest, with other much like; which exercises surely must needs be natural, because they be so childish, and they may be also wholesome for the body; but surely as for pleasure to the mind, or honesty in the doing of them, they be as like shooting as York is foul Sutton. Therefore to look on all pastimes and exercises wholesome for the body, pleasant for the mind, comely for every man to do, honest for all other to look on, profitable to be set by of every man, worthy to be rebuked of no man, fit for all ages, persons, and places, only shooting shall appear, wherein all these commodities may be found.

Phi. To grant, Toxophile, that students may at times convenient use shooting as most wholesome and honest pastime, yet to do as some do, to shoot hourly, daily, weekly, and in a manner the whole year, neither I can praise, nor any wise man will allow, nor you yourself can honestly defend.

Tox. Surely, Philologe, I am very glad to see you come to that point that most lieth in your stomach, and grieveth you and others so much. But I trust, after I have said my mind in this matter, you shall confess yourself that you do rebuke this thing more than you need, rather than you shall find that any man may spend by any possibility, more time in shooting than he ought. For first and foremost, the whole time is divided into two parts, the day and the night; whereof the night may be both occupied in many honest businesses, and also spent in much unthriftiness, but in no wise it can be applied to shooting. And here you see that half our time, granted to all other things in a manner both good and ill, is at one swap quite taken away from shooting. Now let us go forward, and see how much of half this time of ours is spent in shooting. The whole year is divided into four parts, spring-time, summer, fall of the leaf, and winter. Whereof the whole winter, for the roughness of it, is clean taken away from shooting; except it be one day amongst twenty, or one year amongst forty. In summer, for the fervent heat, a man may say likewise ; except it be some time against night. Now then spring-time and fall of the leaf be those which we abuse in shooting.

But if we consider how mutable and changeable the weather is in those seasons, and how that Aristotle himself saith, that most part of rain falleth in these two times; we shall well perceive, that where a man would shoot one day, he shall be fain to leave off four. Now when time itself granteth us but a little space to shoot in, let us see if shooting be not hindered amongst all kinds of men as much other ways.

First, young children use not; young men, for fear of them whom they be under too much, dare not; sage men, for other greater business, will not; aged men, for lack of strength, cannot; rich men, for covetousness sake, care not; poor men, for cost and charge, may not; masters, for their household keeping, heed not; servants, kept in by their masters very oft, shall not; craftsmen, for getting of their living, very much leisure have not; and many there be that oft begins, but, for unaptness, proves not; and most of all, which when they be shooters give it over and list not; so that generally men every where, for one or other consideration, much shooting use not. Therefore these two things, traitness of time, and every man his trade of living, are the causes that so few men shoot, as you may see in this great town, where, as there be a thousand good men's bodies, yet scarce ten that useth any great shooting. And those whom you see shoot the most, with how many things are they drawn, or rather driven, from shooting. For first, as it is many a year or they begin to be great shooters, even so the great heat of shooting is gone within a year or two; as you know divers, Philologe, yourself, which were some time the best shooters, and now they be the best students.

If a man fall sick, farewell shooting, may fortune as long as he liveth. If he have a wrench, or have taken cold in his arm, he may hang up his bow (I warrant you) for a season. A little blain, a small cut, yea a silly poor worm in his finger, may keep him from shooting well enough. Breaking and ill luck in bows I will pass over, with a hundred more serious things, which chanceth everyday to them that shoot most, whereof the least of them may compel a man to leave shooting. And these things be so true and evident, that it is impossible either for me craftily to feign them, or else for you justly to deny them. Then seeing how many hundred things are required altogether to give a man leave to shoot, and, any one of them denied, a man cannot shoot; and seeing every one of them may chance, and doth chance every day; I marvel any wise man will think it possible that any great time can be spent in shooting at all.

Phi. If this be true that you say, Toxophile, and in very deed I can deny nothing of it, I marvel greatly how it chanceth, that those which use shooting be so much marked of men, and oft-times blamed for it, and that in a manner as much as those which play at cards and dice. And I shall tell you what I heard spoken of the same matter. A man, no shooter, (not long ago), would defend playing at cards and dice, if it were honestly used, to be as honest pastime as your shooting; for he laid for him, that a man might play for a little at cards and dice, and also a man might shoot away all that ever he had. He said a pair of cards cost not past two-pence, and that they needed not so much reparation as bow and shafts, they would never hurt a man's hand, nor never wear his gear. A man should never slee [*slay*] a man with shooting wide at the cards. In wet and dry, hot and cold, they would never forsake a man: he showed what great variety there is in them for every man's capacity; if one game were hard, he might easily learn another: if a man have a good game there is great pleasure in it; if he have an ill game the pain is short, for he may soon give it over and hope for a better; with many other mo reasons. But at the last he concluded, that betwixt playing and shooting, well used or ill used, there was no difference; but that there was less cost and trouble, and a great deal more pleasure, in playing than in shooting.

Tox. I cannot deny but shooting (as all other good things) may be abused. And good things ungodly used are not good, saith an honourable bishop in an earnester matter than this is; yet we must be ware that we lay not men's faults upon the thing which is not worthy, for so nothing should be good. And as for shooting, it is blamed and marked of men for that thing (as I said before) which should be rather a token of honesty to praise it, than any sign of naughtiness to disallow it, and that is because it is in every man his sight, it seeketh no corners, it hideth it not; if there be never so little fault in it, every man seeth it, it accuseth itself. For one hour spent in shooting is more seen, and further talked of, than twenty nights spent in dicing, even as a little white stone is seen amongst three hundred black. Of those that blame shooting and shooters, I will say no more at this time but this, that beside that they stop and hinder shooting, which the king's grace would have forward, they be not much unlike in this point to Will Somer the king his fool, which smiteth him that standeth always before his face, be he never so worshipful a man, and never greatly looks for him which lurks behind another man's back, that hurt him in deed.

But to him that compared gaming with shooting somewhat will I answer: and because he went before me in a comparison; and comparisons, saith learned men, make plain matters; I will surely follow him in the same. Honest things (saith Plato) be known from unhonest things by this difference: unhonesty hath ever present pleasure in it, having neither good pretence going before, nor yet any profit following after; which saying, describeth generally both the nature of shooting and gaming, which is good, and which is evil, very well.

Gaming hath joined with it a vain present pleasure; but there followeth loss of name, loss of goods, and winning of an hundred gouty, dropsy, diseases, as every man can tell. Shooting is a painful pastime, whereof followeth health of body, quickness of wit, and ability to defend our country, as our enemies can bear record.

Loth I am to compare these things together, and yet I do it, not because there is any comparison at all betwixt them, but thereby a man shall see how good the one is, how evil the other. For I think there is scarce so much contrariousness betwixt hot and cold, virtue and vice, as is betwixt these two things: for whatsoever is in the one, the clean contrary is in the other, as shall plainly appear, if we consider both their beginnings, their increasings, their fructes, and their ends, which I will soon rid over.

The first bringer into the world of shooting was Apollo, which, for his wisdom, and great commodities brought amongst men by him, was esteemed worthy to be counted as a god in heaven.

Dicing surely is a bastard born, because it is said to have

two fathers, and yet both naught: the one was an ungracious god, called Theuth, which for his naughtiness, came never in other gods' companies, and therefore Homer doth despise once to name him in all his works. The other father was a Lydian born, which people, for such games and other unthriftiness, as bowling and haunting of taverns, have been ever had in most vile reputation in all stories and writers.

The fosterer of shooting is labour, that companion of virtue, the maintainer of honesty, the increaser of health and wealthiness, which admitteth nothing, in a manner, into his company, that standeth not with virtue and honesty; and therefore saith the old poet Epicharmus very prettily in Xenophon, that God selleth virtue and all other good things to men for labour. The nurse of dice and cards is wearisome idleness, enemy of virtue, the drowner of youth that tarrieth in it, and as Chaucer doth say very well in the Parson's Tale, the green path-way to hell, having this thing appropriate unto it, that whereas other vices have some cloak of honesty, only idleness can neither do well nor yet think well. Again, shooting hath two tutors to look upon it, out of whose company shooting never stirreth, the one called Daylight, the other Open Place, which two keep shooting from evil company, and suffers it not to have too much swing, but evermore keeps it under awe, that it dare do nothing in the open face of the world but that which is good and honest. Likewise, dicing and carding have two tutors, the one named solitariousness, which lurketh in holes and corners; the other called night, an ungracious cover of naughtiness, which two things be very inn-keepers and receivers of all naughtiness and naughty things, and thereto they be in a manner ordained by nature. For, on the night time and in corners, spirits and thieves, rats and mice, toads and owls, night-crows and pole-cats, foxes and foumards,* with all other vermin and noisome beasts, use most stirring; when in the day-light and open places, which be ordained of God for honest things, they dare not once come, which thing Euripides noteth very well, saying,

Ill things the night, good things the day, doth haunt and use.

Companions of shooting, be providence, good heed-giving, true meting, honest comparison, which things agree with virtue very well. Carding and dicing have a sort of good fellows also going commonly in their company, as blind fortune, stumbling chance, spittle luck, false dealing, crafty conveyance, brainless brawling, false forswearing; which good fellows will soon take a man by the sleeve and cause him take his inn, some with beggary, some with gout and dropsy, some with theft and robbery, and seldom they will leave a man before he come either to hanging or else some other extreme misery. To make an end, how shooting by all men's laws hath been allowed, carding and dicing by all men's judgments condemned, I need not show, the matter is so plain.

Therefore when the Lydians shall invent better things than

Apollo, when sloth and idleness shall increase virtue more than labour, when the night and-lurking corners giveth less occasion to unthriftiness than light day and openness, then shall shooting and such gaming be in some comparison like. Yet even as I do not show all the goodness which is in shooting, when I prove it standeth by the same things that virtue itself standeth by, as brought in by God or god-like men, fostered by labour, committed to the safeguard of light and openness, accompanied with provision and diligence, loved and allowed by every good man's sentence: even likewise do I not open half the naughtiness which is in carding and dicing, when I show how they are born of a desperate mother, nourished in idleness, increased by licence of night and corners, accompanied with fortune, chance, deceit, and craftiness; condemned and banished by all laws and judgments.

For if I would enter to describe the monstruousness of it, I should rather wander in it, it is so broad, than have any ready passage to the end of the matter; whose horribleness is so large, that it passed the eloquence of our English Homer to compass it; yet because I ever thought his sayings to have as much authority as either Sophocles or Euripides in Greek, therefore gladly do I remember these verses of his:

> Hasardry is very mother of lesings,
> And of deceit, and cursed forswearings;
> Blasphemy of Christ, manslaughter, and

waste also
Of cattle, of time, of other things mo.

Mother of lesings.*] Truly it may well be called so, if a man consider how many ways and how many things he loseth thereby; for first, he loseth his goods, he loseth his time, he loseth quickness of wit, and all good lust to other things; he loseth honest company, he loseth his good name and estimation, and at last, if he leave it not, loseth God and heaven and all; and, instead of these things, winneth at length either hanging or hell.

And of deceit.] I trow, if I should not lie, there is not half so much craft used in no one thing in the world as in this cursed thing. What false dice use they? As dice stopped with quicksilver and hairs, dice of a vantage, flats, gourds to chop and change when they list; to let the true dice fall under the table and so take up the false; and if they be true dice, what shift will they make to set the one of them with sliding, with cogging, with foisting, with quoiting as they call it? How will they use these shifts when they get a plain man that can no skill of them? How will they go about if they perceive an honest man have money, which list not play, to provoke him to play? They will seek his company, they will let him pay nought, yea, and as I heard a man once say that he did, they will send for him to some house and spend perchance a crown on him, and, at last, will one begin to say: What, my masters, what shall we do? shall every man play his twelve-pence whiles an apple roast in the fire, and then we will drink and depart? Nay, will another say (as false as he), you cannot leave when you begin, and therefore I will not play; but if you will gage that every man, as he hath lost his twelve-pence, shall sit down, I am content; for surely I would win no man's money here, but even as much as would pay for my supper. Then speaketh the third to the honest man that thought not to play, What! will you play your twelve-pence? If he excuse him; Tush man, will the other say, stick not in honest company for twelve-pence; I will bear your half, and here is my money.

Now all this is to make him to begin, for they know if he be once in, and be a loser, that he will not stick at his twelve-pence, but hopeth ever to get it again, while perhaps he lose all. Then every one of them setteth his shifts abroach, some with false dice, some with setting of dice, some with having outlandish silver coins gilded to put away at a time for good gold. Then, if there come a thing in controversy, must you be judged by the table, and then farewell the honest man his part, for he is borne down on every side.

Now, Sir, beside all these things, they have certain terms (as a man would say) appropriate to their playing; whereby they will draw a man's money but pay none, which they call bars, that surely he that knoweth them not may soon be debarred of all that ever he hath, afore he learn them. If a plain man lose, as he shall do ever, or else it is a wonder, then the game is so devilish that he can never leave; for vain hope (which hope, saith Euripides, destroyeth many a man and city) driveth him on so far, that he can never return back until he be so light that he need fear no thieves by the way. Now if a simple man happen once in his life to win of such players, then will they either entreat him to keep them company whilst he hath lost all again, or else they will use the most devilish fashion of all, for one of the players that standeth next him shall have a pair of false dice and cast them out upon the board, the honest man shall take them and cast them as he did the other, the third shall espy them to be false dice, and shall cry out hard, with all the oaths under God, that he hath falsely won their money, and then there is nothing but hold thy throat from my dagger; every man layeth hand on the simple man and taketh all their money from him, and his own also, thinking himself well that he escapeth with his life.

Cursed swearing, blasphemy of Christ.] These half verses Chaucer, in another place, more at large doth well set out and very lively express, saying,

> "Ey by Goddes precious heart and by his nails,
> And by the blood of Christ, that is in Hales,
> Seven is my chance, and thine is cinque and trey,
> By Goddes armes, if thou falsely play,

This dagger shall thorough thine hearte go."
This fruit cometh of the beched bones two,
Forswearing, ire, falseness, and homicide, &c.

Though these verses be very earnestly written, yet they do
not half so grisly set out the horribleness of blasphemy which
such gamers use, as it is indeed, and as I have heard myself.
For no man can write a thing so earnestly, as when it is spoken
with gesture, as learned men, you know, do say. How will
you think that such furiousness, with wood countenance, and
brenning eyes, with staring and bragging, with heart ready to
leap out of the belly for swelling, can be expressed the tenth
part to the uttermost. Two men I heard myself, whose sayings
be far more grisly than Chaucer's verses. One when he had
lost his money, sware me God from top to the toe with one
breath, that he had lost all his money for lack of swearing; the
other losing his money and heaping oaths upon oaths one in
another's neck, most horrible and not speakable, was rebuked
of an honest man which stood by for so doing; he, by and
by, staring him in the face, and clapping his fist with all his
money he had upon the board, sware me by the flesh of God,
that, if swearing would help him but one ace, he would not
leave one piece of God unsworn, neither within nor without.
The remembrance of this blasphemy, Philologe, doth make
me quake at the heart, and therefore I will speak no more of
it.

And so to conclude with such gaming, I think there is no ungraciousness in all this world that carrieth a man so far from God as this fault doth. And if there were any so desperate a person that would begin his hell in earth, I trow he should not find hell more like hell itself, than the life of those men is which daily haunt and use such ungracious games.

Phi. You handle this gere indeed; and I suppose, if you had been a prentice at such games, you could not have said more of them than you have done, and by like you have had somewhat to do with them.

Tox. Indeed, you may honestly gather that I hate them greatly, in that I speak against them; not that I have used them greatly, in that I speak of them. For things be known divers ways, as Socrates (you know) doth prove in Alcibiades. And if every man should be that, that he speaketh or written upon, then should Homer have been the best captain, most coward, hardy, hasty, wise and wood, sage and simple; and Terence an old man and a young, an honest man and a bawd; with such like. Surely every man ought to pray to God daily to keep them from such unthriftiness, and especially all the youth of England; for what youth doth begin, a man will follow commonly, even to his dying day; which thing Adrastus, in Euripides, prettily doth express, saying,

What thing a man in tender age hath most in ure,
That same to death always to keep he shall be sure,
Therefore in age who greatly longs good fruit to mow,
In youth he must himself apply good seed to sow.

For the foundation of youth well set (as Plato doth say), the whole body of the commonwealth shall flourish thereafter. If the young tree grow crooked, when it is old a man shall rather break it than straight it. And I think there is no one thing that crooks youth more than such unlawful games. Nor let no man say, if they be honestly used they do no harm. For how can that pastime which neither exerciseth the body with any honest labour, nor yet the mind with any honest thinking, have any honesty joined with it? Nor let no man assure himself that he can use it honestly; for if he stand therein he may fortune have a fall, the thing is more slippery than he knoweth of. A man may (I grant) sit on a brant hill side, but if he give never so little forward, he cannot stop, though he would never so fain, but he must needs run headlong, he knoweth not how far. What honest pretences vain pleasure layeth daily (as it were enticements or baits to pull men forward withal) Homer doth well show by the Sirens and Circes. And amongst all in that ship, there was but one Ulysses, and yet he had done too as the other did, if a goddess had not taught him; and so likewise, I think, they be easy to number which pass by playing honestly, except the grace of God save and keep them. Therefore they that will not go too far in playing, let them follow this counsel of the poet:

Stop the beginnings.

Phi. Well, or you go any further, I pray you tell me this one thing: Do ye speak against mean men's playing only, or against great men's playing too, or put you any difference betwixt them?

Tox. If I should excuse myself herein, and say that I spake of the one and not of the other, I fear lest I should as fondly excuse myself, as a certain preacher did, whom I heard upon a time speak against many abuses (as he said), and, at last, he spake against candles, and then he fearing lest some men would have been angry and offended with him, Nay, saith he, you must take me as I mean: I speak not against great candles, but against little candles, for they be not all one (quoth he), I promise you: and so every man laughed him to scorn.

Indeed, as for great men, and great men's matters, I list not greatly to meddle. Yet this I would wish, that all great men in England had read over diligently the Pardoner's Tale in Chaucer, and there they should perceive and see how much such games stand with their worship, how great soever they be. What great men do, be it good or ill, mean men commonly love to follow, as many learned men in many places do say, and daily experience doth plainly show, in costly apparel and other like matters.

Therefore, seeing that lords be lanterns to lead the life of mean men, by their example, either to goodness or badness, to whither soever they list; and seeing also they have liberty to list what they will, I pray God they have will to list that which is good; and as for their playing, I will make an end with this saying of Chaucer:

> Lords might find them other manner of play,
> Honest enough to drive the day away.

But to be short, the best medicine for all sorts of men, both high and low, young and old, to put away such unlawful games, is by the contrary, likewise as all physicians do allow in physic. So let youth, instead of such unlawful games, which stand by idleness, by solitariness, and corners, by night and darkness, by fortune and chance, by craft and subtilty, use such pastimes as stand by labour, upon the daylight, in open sight of men, having such an end as is come to by cunning, rather than by craft; and so should virtue increase and vice decay. For contrary pastimes must needs work contrary minds in men, as all other contrary things do.

And thus we see, Philologe, that shooting is not only the most wholesome exercise for the body, the most honest pastime for the mind, and that for all sorts of men; but also it is a most ready medicine to purge the whole realm of such pestilent gaming, wherewith many times it is sore troubled and ill at ease.

Phi. The more honesty you have proved by shooting, Toxophile, and the more you have persuaded me to love it, so much truly the sorer have you made me with this last sentence of yours, whereby you plainly prove that a man may not greatly use it. For if shooting be a medicine (as you say that it is), it may not be used very oft, lest a man should hurt himself withal, as medicines much occupied do. For Aristotle himself saith, that medicines be no meat to live withal; and thus shooting, by the same reason, may not be much occupied.

Tox. You play your old wonts, Philologus, in dallying with other men's wits, not so much to prove your own matter, as to prove what other men can say. But where you think that I take away much use of shooting, in likening it to a medicine; because men use not medicines every day, for so should their bodies be hurt; I rather prove daily use of shooting thereby. For although Aristotle saith that some medicines be no meat to live withal, which is true; yet Hippocrates saith that our daily meats be medicines, to withstand evil withal, which is as true; for he maketh two kinds of medicines, one our meat that we use daily, which purgeth softly and slowly, and in this similitude may shooting be called a medicine, wherewith daily a man may purge and take away all unleful desires to other unleful pastimes, as I proved before. The other is a quick purging medicine, and seldomer to be occupied, except the matter be greater; and I could describe the nature of a quick medicine, which should within a while purge and pluck out all the unthrifty games in the realm, through which the commonwealth oftentimes is sick. For not only good quick wits to learning be thereby brought out of frame, and quite marred, but also manly wits, either to attempt matters of high courage in war time, or else to achieve matters of weight and wisdom in peace time, be made thereby very quaisy and faint. For look throughout all histories written in Greek, Latin, or other language, and you shall never find that realm prosper in the which such idle pastimes are used. As concerning the medicine, although some would be miscontent if they heard me meddle any thing with it; yet, betwixt you and me here alone, I may the boldlier say my fantasy, and the rather because I will only wish for it, which standeth with honesty, not determine of it, which belongeth to authority. The medicine is this, that would to God and the king all these unthrifty idle pastimes, which be very bugs that the Psalm meaneth on, walking on the night and in corners, were made felony, and some of that punishment ordained for them which is appointed for the forgers and falsifiers of the King's coin. Which punishment is not by me now invented, but long ago, by the most noble orator Demosthenes, which marvelleth greatly that death is appointed for falsifiers and forgers of the coin, and not as great punishment ordained for them which by their means forges and falsifies the commonwealth. And I suppose that there is no one thing that changeth sooner the golden and silver wits of men into coppery and brassy ways than dicing and such unleful pastimes.

And this quick medicine, I believe, would so thoroughly purge them, that the daily medicines, as shooting and other pastimes, joined with honest labour, should easilier withstand them.

Phi. The excellent commodities of shooting in peace time, Toxophile, you have very well and sufficiently declared. Whereby you have so persuaded me, that, God willing, hereafter I will both love it the better, and also use it the ofter. For as much as I can gather of all this communication of ours, the tongue, the nose, the hands, and the feet, be no fitter members or instruments for the body of a man, than is shooting for the whole body of the realm. God hath made the parts of men which be best and most necessary, to serve, not for one purpose only, but for many; as the tongue for speaking and tasting; the nose for smelling, and also for avoiding all excrements which fall out of the head; the hands for receiving of good things, and for putting of [off] all harmful things from the body. So shooting is an exercise of health, a pastime of honest pleasure, and such one also that stoppeth or avoideth all noisome games, gathered and increased by ill rule, as naughty humours be, which hurt and corrupt sore that part of the realm wherein they do remain.

But now if you can show but half so much profit in war of shooting, as you have proved pleasure in peace, then will

I surely judge that there be few things that have so manifold commodities and uses joined unto them as it hath.

Tox. The upper hand in war, next the goodness of God (of whom all victory cometh, as Scripture saith), standeth chiefly in three things; in the wisdom of the prince, in the sleights and policies of the capitains, and in the strength and cheerful forwardness of the soldiers. A prince in his heart must be full of mercy and peace, a virtue most pleasant to Christ, most agreeable to man's nature, most profitable for rich and poor; for then the rich man enjoyeth with great pleasure that which he hath: the poor may obtain with his labour that which he lacketh. And although there is nothing worse than war,* whereof it taketh his name, through the which great men be in danger, mean men without succour; rich men in fear, because they have somewhat; poor men in care, because they have nothing; and every man in thought and misery: yet it is a civil medicine, wherewith a Prince may, from the body of his commonwealth, put off that danger which may fall, or else recover again whatsoever it hath lost. And therefore, as Isocrates doth say, a Prince must be a warrior in two things, in conning and knowledge of all sleights and feats of war, and in having all necessary habiliments belonging to the same. Which matter to entreat at large, were over-long at this time to declare, and overmuch for my learning to perform.

After the wisdom of the Prince, are valiant capitains most necessary in war, whose office and duty is to know all sleights and policies for all kinds of war, which they may learn two ways, either in daily following and haunting the wars, or else, because wisdom bought with stripes is many time over-costly, they may bestow some time in Vegetius, which entreateth such matters in Latin meetly well; or rather in Polyænus, and Leo the Emperor, which setteth out all policies and duties of capitains in the Greek tongue very excellently. But chiefly I would wish, and (if I were of authority) I would counsel, all the young gentlemen of this realm, never to lay out of their hands two authors, Xenophon in Greek, and Caesar in Latin, wherein they should follow noble Scipio Africanus, as Tully doth say; in which two authors, besides eloquence, a thing most necessary of all other for a captain, they should learn the whole course of war, which those two noble men did not more wisely write for other men to learn, than they did manfully exercise in the field for other men to follow.

The strength of war lieth in the soldier, whose chief praise and virtue is obedience towards his captain, saith Plato. And Xenophon, being a Gentile author, most Christianly doth say, even by these words, that that soldier which first serveth God, and then obeyeth his captain, may boldly, with all courage, hope to overthrow his enemy. Again, without obedience, neither valiant man, stout horse, nor goodly harness, doth any good at all; which obedience of the soldier toward his captain, brought the whole empire of the world into the Romans' hands, and, when it was brought, kept it longer than ever it was kept in any commonwealth before or after. And this to be true, Scipio Africanus, the most noble captain that ever was among the Romans, showed very plainly, what time as he went into Africa to destroy Carthage. For he resting his host by the way in Sicily a day or two and at a time standing with a great man of Sicily, and looking on his soldiers how they exercised themselves in keeping of array, and other feats, the gentleman of Sicily asked Scipio wherein lay his chief hope to overcome Carthage? He answered, In yonder fellows of mine whom you see play. And why? saith the other. Because, saith Scipio, that, if I commanded them to run into the top of this high castle, and cast themselves down backward upon these rocks, I am sure they would do it. Sallust also doth write, that there were more Romans put to death of their captains for setting on their enemies before they had licence, than were for running away out of the field before they had fought. These two examples do prove, that amongst the Romans, the obedience of the soldier was wonderful great, and the severity of the captains to see the same kept, wonderful strait. For they well perceived that an host full of obedience, falleth as seldom into the hands of their enemies, as that body falleth into jeopardy, the which is ruled by reason. Reason and rulers being like in office (for the one ruleth the body of man, the other ruleth the body of the commonwealth), ought to be like of conditions, and ought to be obeyed in all manner of matters. Obedience is nourished by fear and love; fear is kept in by true justice and equity; love is gotten by wisdom, joined with liberality. For where a soldier seeth righteousness so rule, that a man can do neither wrong, nor yet take wrong, and that his captain for his wisdom can maintain him, and for his liberality will maintain him, he must needs both love him and fear him, of the which proceedeth true and unfeigned obedience. After this inward virtue, the next good point in a soldier is to have and to handle his weapon well; whereof the one must be at the appointment of the captain, the other lieth in the courage and exercise of the soldier. Yet of all weapons, the best is, as Euripides doth say, wherewith with least danger of ourself we may hurt our enemy most. And that is (as I suppose) artillery. Artillery, now-a-days, is taken for two things, guns and bows; which, how much they do in war, both daily experience doth teach, and also Peter Nannius, a learned man of Lovain, in a certain dialogue doth very well set out; wherein this is most notable, that when he hath showed exceeding commodities of both, and some discommodities of guns, as infinite cost and charge, cumbersome carriage, and, if they be great, the uncertain levelling, the peril of them that stand by them, the easier avoiding by them that stand far off; and, if they be little, the less both fear and jeopardy is in them, beside all contrary weather and wind, which hindereth them not a little; yet of all shooting he cannot rehearse one discommodity.

Phi. That I marvel greatly at, seeing Nannius is so well learned, and so exercised in the authors of both the tongues;

for I myself do remember that shooting in war is but smally praised, and that of divers captains in divers authors. For first in Euripides, whom you so highly praise (and very well, for Tully thinketh every verse in him to be an authority), what, I pray you, doth Lycus, that overcame Thebes, say as concerning shooting? whose words, as far as I remember, be these, or not much unlike:

What praise hath he at all, which never durst abide,
The dint of a spear's point thrust against his side?
Nor never boldly buckler bore yet in his left hand,
Face to face his enemies' bront stiffly to withstand,
But alway trusteth to a bow, and to a feather'd stick,
Harness ever most fit for him which to fly is quick:
Bow and shaft is armour meetest for a coward,
Which dare not once abide the bront of battle sharp and hard.
    But he a man of manhood most is by mine assent,
Which with heart and courage bold, fully hath him bent
His enemies' look in every stour stoutly to abide,
Face to face, and foot to foot, tide what may betide.

Again, Teucer, the best archer among all the Grecians, in Sophocles, is called of Menelaus a bowman, and a shooter, as in villainy and reproach, to be a thing of no price in war. Moreover, Pandarus, the best shooter in the world, whom Apollo himself taught to shoot, both he and his shooting is quite contemned in Homer, in so much that Homer (which under a made fable doth always hide his judgment of things) doth make Pandarus himself cry out of shooting, and cast his bow away, and take him to a spear, making a vow, that if ever he came home he would break his shafts and burn his bow, lamenting greatly that he was so fond to leave at home his horse and chariot with other weapons, for the trust that he had in his bow. Homer signifying thereby, that men should leave shooting out of war, and take them to other weapons more fit and able for the same; and I trow Pandarus's words be much what after this sort:

> I'll chance, ill luck me hither brought,
> Ill fortune me that day befell,
> When first my bow fro the pin I raught,
> For Hector's sake, the Greeks to quell.
> But if that God so for me shape,
> That home again I may once come,
> Let me never enjoy that hap,
> Nor ever twice look on the sun,
> If bow and shafts I do not burn,
> Which now so evil doth serve my turn.

But to let pass all poets, what can be sorer said against any thing than the judgment of Cyrus is against shooting, which doth cause his Persians, being the best shooters, to lay away their bows and take them to swords and bucklers, spears and darts, and other like hand-weapons'? The which thing Xenophon, so wise a philosopher, so expert a captain in war himself, would never have written, and specially in that book wherein he purposed to show, as Tully saith indeed, not the true history, but the example of a perfect wise Prince and commonwealth, except that judgment of changing artillery into other weapons he had always thought best to be followed in all war. "Whose counsel the Parthians did follow, when they chased Antony over the mountains of Media, which being the best shooters of the world, left their bows and took them to spears and morispikes. And these few examples, I trow, of the best shooters, do well prove that the best shooting is not the best thing, as you call it, in war.

Tox. As concerning your first example, taken out of Euripides, I marvel you will bring it for the dispraise of shooting, seeing Euripides doth make those verses, not because he thinketh them true, but because he thinketh them fit for the person that spake them. For indeed his true judgment of shooting, he doth express by and by after in the oration of the noble captain Amphitryo against Lycus, wherein a man may doubt whether he hath more eloquently confuted Lycus's saying, or more worthily set out the praise of shooting. And as I am advised, his words be much hereafter as I shall say.

Against the witty gift of shooting in a bow,
Fond and lewd words thou lewdly dost out throw,
Which if thou wilt hear of me a word or twain
Quickly thou mayest learn how fondly thou dost blame.
  First, he that with his harness himself doth wall about,
That scarce is left one hole through which he may peep out,
Such bond men to their harness to fight are nothing meet,
But soonest of all other are trodden under feet.
If he be strong, his fellows faint, in whom he putteth his
    trust,
So loaded with his harness he must needs lie in the dust,
Nor yet from death he cannot start, if once his weapon break,
How stout, how strong, how great, how long soever be such a
    freak.
  But whosoever can handle a bow, sturdy, stiff, and strong,
Wherewith like hail many shafts he shoots into the thickest
    throng;
This profit he takes, that standing afar his enemies he may
    spill,
When he and his full safe shall stand, out of all danger and ill.
And this in war is wisdom most, which works our enemies woe,
When we shall be far from all fear and jeopardy of our foe.

Secondarily, even as I do not greatly regard what Menelaus doth say in Sophocles to Teucer, because he spake it both in anger, and also to him that he hated; even so do I remember very well in Homer, that when Hector and the Trojans would have set fire on the Greek ships, Teucer, with his bow, made them recoil back again, when Menelaus took him to his feet and ran away.

Thirdly, as concerning Pandarus, Homer doth not dispraise the noble gift of shooting, but thereby every man is taught, that whatsoever, and how good soever a weapon a man doth use in war, if he be himself a covetous wretch, a fool without counsel, a peace-breaker, as Pandarus was, at last he shall, through the punishment of God, fall into his enemies' hands, as Pandarus did, whom Diomedes, through the help of Minerva, miserably slew.

And, because you make mention of Homer and Troy matters, what can be more praise for any thing, I pray you, than that is for shooting, that Troy could never be destroyed without the help of Hercules shafts, which thing doth signify, that, although all the world were gathered in an army together, yet, without shooting, they can never come to their purpose; as Ulysses, in Sophocles, very plainly doth say unto Pyrrhus, as concerning Hercules shafts to be carried into Troy:

Nor you without them, nor without you they do aught.

Fourthly, whereas Cyrus did change part of his bowmen, whereof he had plenty, into other men of war, whereof he lacked, I will not greatly dispute whether Cyrus did well in that point in those days or no; because it is plain in Xenophon how strong shooters the Persians were, what bows they had, what shafts and heads they occupied, what kind of war their enemies used.

But truly, as for the Parthians, it is plain in Plutarch, that, in changing their bows into spears, they brought their self into utter destruction. For when they had chased the Romans many a mile, through reason of their bows, at the last the Romans, ashamed of their flying, and remembering their old nobleness and courage, imagined this way, that they would kneel down on their knees, and so cover all their body with their shields and targets, that the Parthians' shafts might slide over them, and do them no harm; which thing when the Parthians perceived, thinking that the Romans were forwearied with labour, watch, and hunger, they laid down their bows and took spears in their hands, and so ran upon them; but the Romans perceiving them without their bows, rose up manfully, and slew them every mother's son, save a few that saved themselves with running away. And herein our archers of England far pass the Parthians, which for such a purpose, when they shall come to hand-strokes, hath ever ready, either at his back hanging, or else in his next fellow's hand, a leaden maul, or such-like weapon, to beat down his enemies withal.

Phi. Well, Toxophile, seeing that those examples which I had thought to have been clean against shooting, you have thus turned to the high praise of shooting; and all this praise that you have now said on it, is rather come in by me than sought for of you: let me hear I pray you now, those examples which you have marked of shooting yourself: whereby you are persuaded, and think to persuade others, that shooting is so good in war.

Tox. Examples surely I have marked very many; from the beginning of time had in memory of writing, throughout all commonwealths and empires of the world; whereof the most part I will pass over, lest I should be tedious: yet some I will touch, because they be notable both for me to tell and you to hear.

And because the story of the Jews is for the time most ancient, for the truth most credible, it shall be most fit to begin with them. And although I know that God is the only giver of victory, and not the weapons, for all strength and victory (saith Judas Maccabeus) cometh from Heaven; yet surely strong weapons be the instruments wherewith God doth overcome that part which he will have overthrown. For God is well pleased with wise and witty feats of war: as in meeting of enemies, for truce taking, to have privily in ambushment harnessed men laid for fear of treason, as Judas Maccabeus did with Nicanor, Demetrius captain. And to have engines of war to beat down cities withal; and to have scout watch amongst our enemies to know their counsels, as the noble captain Jonathan, brother to Judas Maccabeus, did in the country of Amathie, against the mighty host of Demetrius. And, beside all this, God is pleased to have goodly tombs for them which do noble feats in war, and to have their images made, and also their coat armours to be set above their tombs, to their perpetual laud and memory! as the valiant captain Simon did cause to be made for his brethren Judas Maccabeus and Jonathan, when they were slain of the Gentiles. And thus, of what authority feats of war and strong weapons be, shortly and plainly we may learn. But amongst the Jews, as I begin to tell, I am sure there was nothing so occupied, or did so much good as bows did; insomuch, that when the Jews had any great upper-hand over the Gentiles, the first thing always that the captain did, was to exhort the people to give all the thanks to God for the victory, and not to their bows, wherewith they had slain their enemies; as it is plain the noble Joshua did after so many kings thrust down by him.

God, when he promiseth help to the Jews, he useth no kind of speaking so much as this, that he will bend his bow and dye his shafts in the Gentiles' blood; whereby it is manifest, that either God will make the Jews shoot strong shoots to overthrow their enemies, or, at least, that shooting is a wonderful mighty thing in war, whereunto the high power of God is likened. David, in the Psalms, calleth bows the vessels of death, a bitter thing, and, in another place, a mighty power, and other ways mo, which I will let pass, because every man readeth them daily; but yet one place of Scripture I must needs remember, which is more notable for the praise of shooting than any that ever I read in any other story: and that is, when Saul was slain of the Philistines, being mighty bowmen, and Jonathas his son with him, that was so good a shooter, as the Scripture saith, that he never shot shaft in vain, and that the kingdom, after Saul's death, came unto David; the first statute and law that ever David made after he was King, was this, that all the children of Israel should learn to shoot, according to a law made many a day before that time, for the setting out of shooting, as it is written (saith Scripture) in *Libro Justorum*, which book we have not now. And thus we see plainly what great use of shooting, and what provision even from the beginning of the world for shooting, was among the Jews.

The Ethiopians, which inhabit the farthest part south in the world, were wonderful bowmen; insomuch that when Cambyses, King of Persia, being in Egypt, sent certain ambassadors into Ethiopia, to the King there, with many great gifts, the King of Ethiope perceiving them to be espies, took them up sharply, and blamed Cambyses greatly for such unjust enterprises; but after that he had princely entertained them, he sent for a bow, and bent it and drew it; and then unbent it again, and said unto the ambassadors, you shall commend me to Cambyses, and give him this bow from me, and bid him, when any Persian can shoot in this bow, let him set upon the Ethiopians; in the mean while let him give thanks unto God, which doth not put in the Ethiopians' minds to conquer any other man's land.

This bow, when it came among the Persians, never one man in such an infinite host (as Herodotus doth say) could stir the string, save only Smerdis, the brother of Cambyses, which stirred it two fingers, and no further; for the which act Cambyses had such envy at him, that he afterward slew him;

as doth appear in the story.

Sesostris, the most mighty King that ever was in Egypt, overcame a great part of the world, and that by archers: he subdued the Arabians, the Jews, the Assyrians: he went farther in Scythia than any man else: he overcame Thracia, even to the borders of Germany. And, in token how he overcame all men, he set up in many places great images to his own likeness, having in the one hand a bow, in the other a sharp-headed shaft; that men might know what weapon his host used in conquering so many people.

Cyrus, counted as a god among the Gentiles, for his nobleness and felicity in war; yet, at the last, when he set upon the Massagetanes, (which people never went without their bow nor their quiver, neither in war nor peace,) he and all his were slain, and that by shooting, as appeareth in the story.

Polycrates, the Prince of Samos (a very little isle), was lord over all the Greek seas, and withstood the power of the Persians, only by the help of a thousand archers.

The people of Scythia, of all other men, loved and used most shooting; the whole riches and household stuff of a man in Scythia was a yoke of oxen, a plough, his nag and his dog, his bow and his quiver; which quiver was covered with the skin of a man, which he took or slew first in battle. The Scythians to be invincible, by reason of their shooting, the great voyages of so many noble conquerors, spent in that country in vain, doth well prove: but specially that of Darius the mighty King of Persia, which, when he had tarried there a great space and done no good, but had for-wearied his host with travail and hunger; at last the men of Scythia sent an ambassador with four gifts, a bird, a frog, a mouse, and five shafts. Darius, marvelling at the strangeness of the gifts, asked the messenger what they signified: the messenger answered, that he had no further commandment, but only to deliver his gifts and return again with all speed: "But I am sure," saith he, "you Persians for your great wisdom can soon bolt out what they mean." When the messenger was gone, every man began to say his verdict. Darius judgment was this: that the Scythians gave over into the Persians hands their lives, their whole power both by land and sea, signifying by the mouse the earth, by the frog the water, in which they both live, by the bird their lives which live in the air; by the shaft their whole power and empire, that was maintained always by shooting. Gobryas, a noble and wise captain among the Persians, was of a clean contrary mind, saying, "Nay, not so, but the Scythians mean thus by their gifts; that except we get us wings, and fly into the air like birds, or run into the holes of the earth like mice, or else lie lurking in fens and marshes like frogs, we shall never return home again, before we be utterly undone with their shafts: "which sentence sank so sore into their hearts, that Darius, with all speed possible, brake up his camp and got himself homeward. Yet how much the Persians themselves set by shooting, whereby they increased their empire so much, doth appear by three manifest reasons: First, that they brought up their youth in the school of shooting under twenty year of age, as divers noble Greek authors do say.

Again, because the noble King Darius thought himself to be praised by nothing so much as to be counted a good shooter, as doth appear by his sepulchre, wherein he caused to be written this sentence:

> Darius the King lieth buried
> here,
> That in shooting and riding
> had never peer.

Thirdly, the coin of the Persians, both gold and silver, had the arms of Persia upon it, as is customably used in other realms, and that was bow and arrows; by the which feat they declared how much they set by them.

The Grecians also, but specially the noble Athenians, had all their strength lying in artillery; and, for that purpose, the city of Athens had a thousand men, which were only archers, in daily wages, to watch and keep the city from all jeopardy and sudden danger; which archers also should carry to prison and ward any misdoer at the commandment of the high officers, as plainly doth appear in Plato. And surely the bowmen of Athens did wonderful feats in many battles, but specially when Demosthenes, the valiant captain, slew and took prisoners all the Lacedaemonians, beside the city of Pylos, where Nestor some time was lord: the shafts went so thick that day (saith Thucydides) that no man could see their enemies. A Lacedaemonian, taken prisoner, was asked of one at Athens, whether they were stout fellows that were slain or no, of the Lacedaemonians? He answered nothing else but this: "Make much of those shafts of yours, for they know neither stout nor unstout;" meaning thereby, that no man (though he were never so stout) came in their walk that escaped without death.

Herodotus, describing the mighty host of Xerxes, especially doth mark out what bows and shafts they used, signifying that therein lay their chief strength. And at the same time Atossa, mother of Xerxes, wife to Darius, and daughter of Cyrus, doth enquire (as Æschylus showeth in a tragedy) of a certain messenger that came from Xerxes host, what strong and fearful bows the Grecians used: whereby it is plain, that artillery was the thing wherein both Europe and Asia in those days trusted most upon.

The best part of Alexander's host were archers, as plainly doth appear by Arrianus, and other that wrote his life; and those so strong archers, that they only, sundry times overcame their enemies afore any other needed to fight; as was seen in the battle which Nearchus, one of Alexander's captains, had beside the river Thomeron. And therefore, as concerning all these kingdoms and commonwealths, I may conclude with this sentence of Pliny, whose words be, as I suppose, thus: "If any man would remember the Ethiopians, Egyptians, Arabians, the men of Inde, of Scythia, so many people in the east of the Sarmatians, and all the kingdoms of the Parthians, he shall well perceive half the part of the world to live in subjection, overcome by the might and power of shooting."

In the commonwealth of Home, which exceeded all other in virtue, nobleness, and dominion, little mention is made of shooting, not because it was little used amongst them, but rather because it was so necessary and common, that it was thought a thing not necessary or required of any man to be spoken upon; as if a man should describe a great feast, he would not once name bread, although it be most common and necessary of all; but surely, if a feast, being never so great, lacked bread, or had fusty and naughty bread, all the other dainties should be unsavory and little regarded, and then would men talk of the commodity of bread, when they lack it, that would not once name it afore, when they had it; and even so did the Romans, as concerning shooting. Seldom is shooting named, and yet it did the most good in war, as did appear very plainly in that battle which Scipio Africanus had with the Numantines in Spain, whom he could never overcome, before he set bowmen amongst his horsemen, by whose might they were clean vanquished.

Again, Tiberius, fighting with Arminus and In-guiomerus,

princes of Germany, had one wing of archers on horseback, another of archers on foot, by whose might the Germans were slain downright, and so scattered and beat out of the field, that the chase lasted ten miles; the Germans clame up into trees for fear, but the Romans did fetch them down with their shafts, as they had been birds, in which battle the Romans lost few or none, as doth appear in the history.

But, as I began to say, the Romans did not so much praise the goodness of shooting when they had it, as they did lament the lack of it when they wanted it; as Leo V, the noble Emperor, doth plainly testify in sundry places, in those books which he wrote in Greek, of the sleights and policies of war.

Phi. Surely of that book I have not heard before; and how came you to the sight of it?

Tox. The book is rare truly; but this last year, when Master Cheke translated the said book out of Greek into Latin, to the King's Majesty, he, of his gentleness, would have me very oft in his chamber, and, for the familiarity that I had with him, more than many other, would suffer me to read of it, when I would; the which thing to do surely I was very desirous and glad, because of the excellent handling of all things that ever he taketh in hand. And verily, Philologe, as oft as I remember the departing of that man from the University, (which thing I do not seldom), so oft do I well perceive our most help and furtherance to learning, to have gone away with him. For, by the great commodity that we took in hearing him read privately in his chamber, all Homer, Sophocles, and Euripides, Herodotus, Thucy-dides, Xenophon, Isocrates, and Plato, we feel the great discommodity in not hearing of him Aristotle and Demosthenes, which two authors, with all diligence, last of all, he thought to have read unto us. And when I consider how many men be succoured with his help, and his aid to abide here for learning, and how all men were provoked and stirred up by his counsel and daily example how they should come to learning, surely I perceive that sentence of Plato to be true, which sayeth: "that there is nothing better in any commonwealth, than that there should be always one or other excellent passing man, whose life and virtue should pluck forward the will, diligence, labour, and hope of all other; that, following his footsteps, they might come to the same end, whereunto labour, learning, and virtue had conveyed him before."

The great hinderance of learning, in lacking this man, greatly I should lament, if this discommodity of ours were not joined with the commodity and health of the whole realm; for which purpose our noble King, full of wisdom, called up this excellent man, full of learning, to teach noble Prince Edward; an office full of hope, comfort, and solace to all true hearts of England; for whom all England daily doth pray, that he, passing his tutor in learning and knowledge, following his father in wisdom and felicity, according to that example which is set afore his eyes, may so set out and maintain God's word, to the abolishment of all papistry, the confusion of all heresy, that thereby he, feared of his enemies, loved of all his subjects, may bring to his own glory immortal fame and memory, to this realm wealth, honour, and felicity, to true and unfeigned religion perpetual peace, concord, and unity.

But to return to shooting again, what Leo saith of shooting amongst the Romans; his words be so much for the praise of shooting, and the book also so rare to be gotten, that I learned the places by heart, which be as I suppose, even thus. First, in his sixth book, as concerning what harness is best: "Let all the youth of Rome be compelled to use shooting, either more or less, and always to bear their bow and their quiver about with them, until they be eleven years old. For since shooting was neglected and decayed among the Romans, many a battle and field hath been lost." Again, in the eleventh book and fiftieth chapter (I call that by books and chapiters, which the Greek book divideth by chapiters and paragraphs): "Let your soldiers have their weapons well appointed and trimmed; but, above all other things, regard most shooting; and therefore let men, when there is no war, use shooting at home. For the leaving off only of shooting, hath brought in ruin and decay the whole empire of Rome."

Afterward he commandeth again his capitain by these words: "Arm your host as I have appointed you, but specially with bow and arrows plenty. For shooting is a thing of much might and power in war, and chiefly against the Saracens and

Turks, which people hath all their hope of victory in their bow and shafts." Besides all this, in another place, he writeth thus to his captain: "Artillery is easy to be prepared, and, in time of great need, a thing most profitable, therefore we straitly command you to make proclamation to all men under our dominion, which be either in war or peace, to all cities, boroughs, and towns, and finally, to all manner of men, that every sere person have bow and shafts of his own, and every house beside this to have a standing bearing bow, and forty shafts for all needs, and that they exercise themselves in holts, hills, and dales, plains and woods, for all manner of chances in war."

How much shooting was used among the old Romans, and what means noble captains and emperors made to have it increase amongst them, and what hurt came by the decay of it, these words of Leo the Emperor, which, in a manner, I have rehearsed word for word, plainly doth declare.

And yet shooting, although they set never so much by it, was never so good then as it is now in England; which thing to be true is very probable, in that Leo doth say, "That he would have his soldiers take off their arrow heads, and one shoot at another, for their exercise;" which play if English archers used, I think they should find small play, and less pleasure in it at all.

The great upperhand maintained always in war by artillery, doth appear very plainly by this reason also, that when the

Spaniards, Frenchmen, and Germans, Greeks, Macedonians, and Egyptians, each country using one singular weapon, for which they were greatly feared in war, as the Spaniard Lancea, the Frenchman Gesa, the German Framea, the Grecian Machera, the Macedonian Sarissa, yet could they not escape but be subjects to the empire of Rome; when the Parthians, having all their hope in artillery, gave no place to them, but overcame the Romans oftener than the Romans them, and kept battle with them many a hundred year, and slew the rich Crassus and his son, with many a stout Roman more, with their bows; they drave Marcus Antonius over the hills of Media in Armenia, to his great shame and reproach; they slew Julianus the apostate, and Antoninus Caracalla; they held in perpetual prison the most noble Emperor Valerian, in despite of all the Romans and many other princes which wrote for his deliverance, as Bel solis, called King of Kings, Valerius King of Cadusia, Arthabesdes King of Armenia, and many other princes more, whom the Parthians, by reason of their artillery, regarded never one whit; and thus with the Romans, I may conclude, that the borders of their empire were not at the sun-rising and sun-setting, as Tully saith; but so far they went, as artillery would give them leave. For, I think, all the ground that they had, either northward, further than the borders of Scythia, or eastward, further than the borders of Parthia, a man might have bought with a small deal of money; of which thing surely shooting was the cause.

From the same country of Scythia, the Goths, Huns, and Vandalians came with the same weapons of artillery, as Paulus Diaconus doth say, and so bereft Rome of her empire by fire, spoil, and waste; so that in such a learned city was left scarce one man behind, that had learning or leisure to leave in writing to them which should come after, how so noble an empire, in so short a while, by a rabble of banished bondmen, without all order and policy, save only their natural and daily exercise in artillery, was brought to such thraldom and ruin.

After them the Turks, having another name, but yet the same people, born in Scythia, brought up only in artillery, by the same weapon have subdued and bereft from the Christian men all Asia and Africa (to speak upon) and the most noble countries of Europe, to the great diminishing of Christ his religion, to the great reproach of cowardice of all Christianity, a manifest token of God's high wrath and displeasure over the sin of the world, but specially amongst Christian men, which be on sleep, made drunk with the fruits of the flesh, as infidelity, disobedience to God's word, and heresy, grudge, ill-will, strife, open battle, and privy envy, covetousness, oppression, unmercifulness, with innumerable sorts of unspeakable daily bawdry; which things surely, if God hold not his holy hand over us, and pluck us from them, will bring us to a more Turkishness, and more beastly blind barbarousness, as calling ill things good, and good things ill, contemning of knowledge and learning, setting at nought, and having for a fable, God and his high providence, will bring us, I say, to a more ungracious Turkishness, if more Turkishness can be than this, than if the Turks had sworn to bring all Turkey against us. For these fruits surely must needs spring of such seed, and such effect needs follow of such a cause, if reason, truth, and God be not altered, but as they are wont to be. For surely no Turkish power can overthrow us, if Turkish life do not cast us down before. If God were with us, it booted not the Turk to be against us; but our unfaithful sinful living, which is the Turk's mother, and hath brought him up hitherto, must needs turn God from us, because sin and he hath no fellowship together. If we banished ill-living out of Christendom, I am sure the Turk should not only not overcome us, but scarce have an hole to run into in his own country.

But Christendom now, I may tell you, Philologe, is much like a man that hath an itch on him, and lieth drunk also in his bed, and though a thief come to the door, and heaveth at it, to come in and slay him, yet he lieth in his bed, having more pleasure to lie in a slumber and scratch himself where it itcheth, even to the hard bone, than he hath readiness to rise up lustily, and drive him away that would rob him and slay him. But, I trust, Christ will so lighten and lift up Christian men's eyes, that they shall not sleep to death, nor that the Turk, Christ's open enemy, shall ever boast that he hath quite overthrown us.

But, as I began to tell you, shooting is the chief thing

wherewith God suffereth the Turk to punish our naughty living withal: the youth there is brought up in shooting, his privy guard for his own person is bowmen, the might of their shooting is well known of the Spaniards, which at the town called Newcastle, in Illyrica, were quite slain up of the Turk's arrows, when the Spaniards had no use of their guns by reason of the rain. And now, last of all, the Emperor his Majesty himself, at the city of Argier in Afrike, had his host sore handled with the Turks' arrows, when his guns were quite dispatched, and stood him in no service because of the rain that fell; whereas, in such a chance of rain, if he had had bowmen, surely their shot might peradventure have been a little hindered, but quite dispatched and marred it could never have been. But, as for the Turks, I am weary to talk of them, partly because I hate them, and partly because I am now affectioned even as it were a man that had been long wandering in strange countries, and would fain be at home to see how well his own friends prosper and lead their life. And surely, methink, I am very merry at my heart to remember how I shall find at home in England, amongst Englishmen, partly by histories of them that have gone afore us, again by experience of them, which we know and live with us, as great noble feats of war done by artillery as ever was done at any time in any other commonwealth. And here I must needs remember a certain Frenchman, called Textor, that writeth a book which he nameth Officina, wherein he weaveth up many broken ended matters, and sets

out much riffraff, pelfery, trumpery, baggage, and beggary
ware, clamparde up of one that would seem to be fitter for a
shop indeed than to write any book. And, amongst all other
ill-packed up matters, he thrusts up in a heap together all the
good shooters that ever hath been in the world, as he saith
himself; and yet I trow, Philologe, that all the examples which
I now, by chance, have rehearsed out of the best authors both
in Greek and Latin, Textor hath but two of them, which two
surely, if they were to reckon again, I would not once name
them, partly because they were naughty persons, and shooting
so much the worse because they loved it, as Domitian and
Commodus, the Emperors; partly because Textor hath them
in his book, on whom I looked by chance in the book-binder's
shop, thinking of no such matter. And one thing I will say
to you, Philologus, that if I were disposed to do it, and you
had leisure to hear it, I could soon do as Textor doth, and
reckon up such a rabble of shooters, that be named here and
there in poets, as would hold us talking whilst to-morrow;
but my purpose was not to make mention of those which
were feigned of poets for their pleasure, but of such as were
proved in histories for a truth. But why I bring in Textor was
this: At last, when he hath reckoned all shooters that he can,
he saith thus, Petrus Crinitus writeth, that the Scots, which
dwell beyond England, be very excellent shooters, and the
best bowmen in war. This sentence, whether Crinitus wrote
it more lewdly of ignorance, or Textor confirmeth it more

peevishly of envy, may be called in question and doubt, but this surely do I know very well, that Textor hath both read in Gaguinus the French history, and also hath heard his father or grandfather talk (except perchance he was born and bred in a cloister) after that sort of the shooting of Englishmen, that Textor needed not to have gone so peevishly beyond England for shooting, but might very soon, even in the first town of Kent, have found such plenty of shooting, as is not in all the realm of Scotland again. The Scots surely be good men of war in their own feats as can be; but as for shooting, they neither can use it for any profit, nor yet will challenge it for any praise, although Master Textor, of his gentleness, would give it them. Textor needed not to have filled up his book with such lies, if he had read the history of Scotland, which Johannes Major doth write; wherein he might have learned, that when James Stewart, first king of that name, at the parliament holden at Saint John's town, or Perthie, commanding under pain of a great forfeit, that every Scot should learn to shoot; yet neither the love of their country, the fear of their enemies, the avoiding of punishment, nor the receiving of any profit that might come by it, could make them to be good archers which be unapt and unfit thereunto by God's providence and nature.

Therefore the Scots themselves prove Textor a liar, both with authority and also daily experience, and by a certain proverb that they have amongst them in their communication, whereby they give the whole praise of shooting honestly to Englishmen, saying thus : that "every English archer beareth under his girdle twenty four Scots."

But to let Textor and the Scots go, yet one thing would I wish for the Scots, and that is this; that seeing one God, one faith, one compass of the sea, one land and country, one tongue in speaking, one manner and trade in living, like courage and stomach in war, like quickness of wit to learning, hath made England and Scotland both one, they would suffer them no longer to be two; but clean give over the pope, which seeketh none other thing (as many a noble and wise Scottish man doth know) but to feed up dissension and parties betwixt them and us, procuring that thing to be two, which God, nature, and reason would have one.

How profitable such an atonement* were for Scotland, both Johannes Major and Hector Boetius, which wrote the Scots Chronicles, do tell, and also all the gentlemen of Scotland, with the poor commonalty, do well know; so that there is nothing that stoppeth this matter, save only a few freers [*friars*] and such like, which, with the dregs of our English Papistry lurking amongst them, study nothing else but to brew battle and strife betwixt both the people; whereby only they hope to maintain their papistical kingdom, to the destruction of the noble blood of Scotland, that then they may with authority do that, which neither noble man nor poor man in Scotland yet doth know. And as [for]* Scottish men and English men be not enemies by nature, but by custom; not by our good will, but by their own folly; which should take more honour in being coupled to England, than we should take profit in being joined to Scotland.

Wales being heady, and rebelling many years against us, lay wild, untilled, uninhabited, without law, justice, civility, and order; and then was amongst them more stealing than true dealing, more surety for them than studied to be naught, than quietness for them that laboured to be good; when now, thanked be God and noble England, there is no country better inhabited, more civil, more diligent in honest crafts, to get both true and plentiful living withal. And this felicity (my mind giveth me) shall chance also to Scotland, by the godly wisdom of our most noble prince King Henry VIII, by whom God hath wrought more wonderful things than ever by any prince before; as banishing the bishop of Home and heresy, bringing to light God's word and verity, establishing such justice and equity through every part of this his realm, as never was seen afore.

To such a prince of such a wisdom, God hath reserved this most noble atonement; whereby neither we shal be any more troubled, nor the Scots with their best countries any more destroyed, nor the sea, which God ordained profitable for both, shall from either be any more stopped; to the great quietness, wealth, and felicity of all the people dwelling in this isle, to the high renown and praise of our most noble king, to the fear of all manner of nations that owe ill will to either country, to the high pleasure of God, which as he is one, and hateth all divisions, so is he best of all pleased to see things which be wide and amiss, brought to peace and atonement.*

But Textor (I beshrew him) hath almost brought us from our communication of shooting. Now, sir, by my judgment, the artillery of England far exceedeth all other realms : but yet one thing I doubt, and long have surely in that point doubted, when, or by whom, shooting was first brought into England; and, for the same purpose, as I was once in company with Sir Thomas Eliot, knight, (which surely for his learning in all kind of knowledge, brought much worship to all the nobility of England,) I was so bold to ask him, if he at any time had marked any thing, as concerning the bringing in of shooting into England: he answered me gently again, he had a work in hand, which he nameth, *De rebus memorabilibus Angliæ*, which I trust we shall see in print shortly, and, for the accomplishment of that book, he had read and perused over many old Monuments of England; and, in seeking for that purpose, he marked this of shooting in an exceeding old chronicle, the which had no name, that what time as the Saxons came first into this realm, in King Vortiger's days, when they had been here a while, and at last began to fall out with the Britons, they troubled and subdued the Britons with nothing so much as with their bow and shafts, which weapon being strange and not seen here before, was wonderful terrible unto them; and this beginning I can think very well to be true. But now as concerning many examples for the praise of English archers in war, surely I will not be long in a matter that no man doubteth in; and those few that I will name, shall either be proved by the history of our enemies, or else done by men that now live.

King Edward III, at the battle of Cressy, against Philip the French King, as Gaguinus the French historiographer, plainly doth tell, slew that day all the nobility of France only with his archers.

Such like battle also fought the noble Black Prince Edward, beside Poictiers, where John the French King, with his son, and in a manner all the peers of France were taken, beside 30,000 which that day were slain, and very few English men, by reason of their bows.

King Henry V, a prince peerless, and most victorious conqueror of all that ever died yet in this part of the world, at the battle of Dagincourt, with seven thousand fighting men, and yet many of them sick, being such archers, as the chronicle saith, that most part of them drew a yard, slew all the chivalry of France, to the number of forty thousand and moo, and lost not past twenty-six Englishmen.

The bloody civil war of England betwixt the house of York and Lancaster, where shafts flew of both sides to the destruction of many a yeoman of England, whom foreign battle could never have subdued, both I will pass over for the pitifulness of it, and yet may we highly praise God in the remembrance of it, seeing he, of his providence, hath so knit together those two noble houses, with so noble and pleasant a flower.

The excellent prince Thomas Howard duke of North-folk (for whose good prosperity with all his noble family all English hearts daily doth pray),* with bow men of England, slew King Jamie with many a noble Scot, even brant against Flodden Hill; in which battle the stout archers of Cheshire and Lancashire, for one day bestowed to the death for their prince and country sake, hath gotten immortal name and praise for ever.

The fear only of English archers hath done more wonderful things than ever I read in any history, Greek or Latin, and most wonderful of all now of late, beside Carlisle, betwixt Esk and Leven, at Sandysikes, where the whole nobility of Scotland, for fear of the archers of England, (next the stroke of God,) as both English and Scottish men that were present that told me, were drowned and taken prisoners.

Nor that noble act also, which although it be almost lost by time, cometh not behind in worthiness, which my singular good friend and master Sir William Walgrave, and Sir George Somerset did, with a few archers, to the number, as it is said, of sixteen, at the turnpike beside Hammes, where they turned with so few archers so many Frenchmen to flight, and turned so many out of their jacks;† which turn turned all France to shame and reproach, and those two noble knights to perpetual praise and fame.

And thus you see, Philologe, in all countries, Asia, Afrike, and Europe, in Inde, Ethiop, Egypt, and Jewry, Parthia, Persia, Greece and Italy, Scythia, Turkey, and England, from the beginning of the world even to this day, that shooting hath had the chief stroke in war.

Phi. These examples surely, apt for the praise of shooting, not feigned by poets, but proved by true histories, distinct by time and order, hath delighted me exceeding much; but yet methink that all this praise belongeth to strong shooting and drawing of mighty bows, not to pricking and near shooting, for which cause you and many other both love and use shooting.

Tox. Evermore, Philologe, you will have some over-thwart reason to draw forth more communication withal; but, nevertheless, you shall perceive if you will, that use of pricking, and desire of near shooting at home, are the only causes of strong shooting in war, and why? For you see that the strongest men do not draw always the strongest shot, which thing proveth that drawing strong lieth not so much in the strength of man, as in the use of shooting. And experience teacheth the same in other things, for you shall see a weak smith, which will, with a lipe* and turning of his arm take up a bar of iron, that another man, thrice as strong, cannot stir. And a strong man, not used to shoot, hath his arms, breast, and shoulders, and other parts wherewith he should draw strongly, one hindering and stopping another, even as a dozen strong horses not used to the cart, lets and troubles one another. And so the more strong man, not used to shoot, shoots most unhandsomely ; but yet if a strong man with use of shooting could apply all the parts of his body together, to their most strength, then should he both draw stronger than other, and also shoot better than other. But now a strong man, not used to shoot, at a gird can heave up and pluck in sunder many a good bow, as wild horses at a brunt doth race and pluck in pieces many a strong cart. And thus strong men, without use, can do nothing in shooting to any purpose, neither in war nor peace; but if they happen to shoot, yet they have done within a shot or two, when a weak man that is used to shoot, shall serve for all times and purposes, and shall shoot ten shafts against the other's four, and draw them up to the point every time, and shoot them to the most advantage, drawing and withdrawing his shaft when he list, marking at one man, yet let driving at another man; which things, in a set battle, although a man shall not always use, yet in bickerings, and at overthwart meetings, when few archers be together, they do most good of all.

Again, he that is not used to shoot, shall evermore with untowardness of holding his bow, and knocking his shaft, not looking to his string betime, put his bow always in jeopardy of breaking, and then he were better to be at home : moreover he shall shoot very few shafts, and those full unhandsomely, some not half drawn, some too high, and some too low; nor he cannot drive a shot at a time, nor stop a shot at a need, but out must it, and very oft to evil proof.

Phi. And that is best, I trow, in war, to let it go, and not to stop it.

Tox. No, not so, but some time to hold a shaft at the head; which, if they be but few archers, doth more good with the fear of it, than it should do if it were shot with the stroke of it.

Phi. That is a wonder to me, that the fear of a displeasure should do more harm than the displeasure itself.

Tox. Yes, ye know that a man which feareth to be banished out of his country, can neither be merry, eat, drink, nor sleep for fear; yet when he is banished indeed, he sleepeth and eateth as well as any other. And many men, doubting and fearing whether they should die or no, even for very fear of death, preventeth themselves with a more bitter death than the other death should have been indeed. And thus fear is ever worse than the thing feared, as is prettily proved by the communication of Cyrus and Tigranes, the King's son of Armenie, in Xenophon.

Phi. I grant, Toxophile, that use of shooting maketh a man draw strong, to shoot at most advantage, to keep his gear, which is no small thing in war; but yet methink that the customable shooting at home, specially at butts and pricks, make nothing at all for strong shooting, which doth most good in war. Therefore, I suppose, if men should use to go into the fields, and learn to shoot mighty strong shots, and never care for any mark at all, they should do much better.

Tox. The truth is, that fashion much used would do much good, but this is to be feared, lest that way could not provoke men to use much shooting, because there should be little pleasure in it. And that in shooting is best, that provoketh a man to use shooting most; for much use maketh men shoot both strong and well, which two-things in shooting every man doth desire. And the chief maintainer of use in any thing is comparison and honest contention. For when a man striveth to be better than another, he will gladly use that thing, though it be never so painful, wherein he would excel; which thing Aristotle very prettily doth note, saying, "Where is comparison, there is victory; where is victory, there is pleasure; and where is pleasure, no man careth what labour or pain he taketh, because of the praise and pleasure that he shall have in doing better than other men."

Again, you know, Hesiodus writeth to his brother Perses, "that all craftsmen, by contending one honestly with another, do increase their cunning with their substance." And therefore in London, and other great cities, men of one craft, most commonly, dwell together, because in honest striving together who shall do best, every one may wax both cunninger and richer. So likewise in shooting, to make matches, to assemble archers together, to contend who shall shoot best, and win the game, increaseth the use of shooting wonderfully amongst men.

Phi. Of use you speak very much, Toxophile; but I am sure in all other matters use can do nothing without two other things be joined with it; one is a natural aptness to a thing, the other is a true way or knowledge how to do the thing; to which two if use be joined as third fellow of them three, proceedeth perfectness and excellency : if a man lack the first two, aptness and cunning, use can do little good at all.

For he that would be an orator, and is nothing naturally fit for it, that is to say, lacketh a good wit and memory, lacketh a good voice, countenance, and body, and other such like; yea, if he had all these things, and knew not what, how, where, when, nor to whom he should speak; surely the use of speaking would bring out none other fruit but plain folly and babbling; so that use is the last and the least necessary of all three, yet nothing can be done excellently without them all three; and therefore, Toxophile, I myself, because I never knew whether I was apt for shooting or no, nor never knew way how I should learn to shoot, I have not used to shoot; and so, I think, five hundred more in England do beside me. And surely, if I knew that I were apt, and that you would teach me how to shoot, I would become an archer; and the rather because of the good communication, the which I have had with you this day of shooting.

Tox. Aptness, knowledge, and use, even as you say, make all things perfect. Aptness is the first and chiefest thing, without which the other two do no good at all. Knowledge doth increase all manner of aptness both less and more. "Use," saith Cicero, "is far above all teaching." And thus they all three must be had, to do any thing very well; and if any one be away, whatsoever is done, is done very meanly. Aptness is the gift of nature, knowledge is gotten by the help of other; use lieth in our own diligence and labour; so that aptness and use be ours and within us, through nature and labour; knowledge not ours, but coming by other; and therefore most diligently of all men to be sought for. How these three things stand with the artillery of England, a word or two I will say.

All Englishmen, generally, be apt for shooting; and how? Like as that ground is plentiful and fruitful, which, without any tilling, bringeth out corn: as, for example, if a man should go to the mill or market with corn, and happen to spill some in the way, yet it would take root and grow, because the soil is so good; so England may be thought very fruitful, and apt to bring out shooters, where children, even from the cradle, love it, and young men, without any teaching, so diligently use it. Again, likewise as a good ground, well tilled and well husbanded, bringeth out great plenty of big-eared corn, and good to the fall: so if the youth of England, being apt of itself to shoot, were taught and learned how to shoot, the archers of England should not be only a great deal ranker, and mo than they be; but also a good deal bigger and stronger archers than they be. This commodity should follow also, if the youth of England were taught to shoot, that even as ploughing of a good ground for wheat, doth not only make it meet for the seed, but also riveth and plucketh up by the roots all thistles, brambles, and weeds, which grow of their own accord, to the destruction of both corn and ground : even so should the teaching of youth to shoot, not only make them shoot well, but also pluck away by the roots all other desire to naughty pastimes, as dicing, carding, and bowling, which, without any teaching, are used every where, to the great harm of all youth of this realm. And likewise as burning of thistles, and diligent weeding them out of the corn, doth not half so much rid them, as when the ground is fallowed and tilled for good grain, as I have heard many a good husbandman say: even so, neither hot punishment, nor yet diligent searching out of such unthrifti-ness by the officers, shall so thoroughly weed these ungracious games out of the realm, as occupying and bringing up youth in shooting, and other honest pastime. Thirdly, as a ground which is apt for corn, and also well tilled for corn; yet if a man let it lie still, and do not occupy it three or four year; but then will sow it, if it be wheat, saith Columella, it will turn into rye: so if a man be never so apt to shoot, nor never so well taught in his youth to shoot, yet if he give it over, and not use to shoot, truly when he shall be either compelled in war time for his country sake, or else provoked at home for his pleasure sake, to fall to his bow, he shall become, of a fair archer, a stark squirter and dribber. Therefore, in shooting, as in all other things, there can neither be many in number, nor excellent in deed, except these three things, aptness, knowledge, and use, go together.

Phi. Very well said, Toxophile; and I promise you, I agree to this judgment of yours together; and therefore I cannot a little marvel, why Englishmen bring no more help to shooting than nature itself giveth them. For you see that even children be put to their own shifts in shooting, having nothing taught them; but that they may choose, and chance to shoot ill rather than well, unaptly sooner than fitly, untowardly more easily than well-favouredly; which thing causeth many never to begin to shoot, and moo to leave it off when they have begun; and most of all to shoot both worse and weaker than they might shoot, if they were taught.

But peradventure some men will say, that with use of shooting a man shall learn to shoot: true it is, he shall learn, but what shall he learn? Marry to shoot naughtily. For all use, in all things, if it be not stayed by cunning, will very easily bring a man to do the thing, whatsoever he goeth about, with much ill-favouredness and deformity. Which thing how much harm it doth in learning, both Crassus excellently doth prove in Tully, and I myself have experience in my little shooting. And therefore, Toxophile, you must needs grant me, that either Englishmen do ill in not joining knowledge of shooting to use, or else there is no knowledge or cunning which can be gathered of shooting.

Tox. Learning to shoot is little regarded in England, for this consideration, because men be so apt by nature, they have a great ready forwardness and will to use it, although no man teach them, although no man bid them; and so of their own courage they run headlong on it, and shoot they ill, shoot they well, great heed they take not. And, in very deed, aptness with use may do somewhat without knowledge, but not the tenth part, if so be they were joined with knowledge. Which three things be separate as you see, not of their own kind, but through the negligence of men which coupled them not together. And where ye doubt, whether there, can be gathered any knowledge or art in shooting or no, surely I think that a man, being well exercised in it, and somewhat honestly learned withal, might soon, with diligent observing and marking the whole nature of shooting, find out, as it were, an art of it, as arts in other matters have been found out afore; seeing that shooting standeth by those things, which may both be thoroughly perceived, and perfectly known, and such that never fails, but be ever certain, belonging to one most perfect end; as shooting straight and keeping of a length bring a man to hit the mark, the chief end in shooting, which two things a man may attain unto, by diligent using and well-handling those instruments which belong unto them. Therefore I cannot see, but there lieth hid in the nature of shooting an art, which by noting and observing of him that is exercised in it, if he be any thing learned at all, may be taught, to the great furtherance of artillery throughout all this realm; and truly I marvel greatly, that Englishmen would never yet seek for the art of shooting, seeing they be so apt unto it, so praised of their friends, so feared of their enemies for it. Vegetius would have masters appointed, which should teach youth to shoot fair. Leo the Emperor of Rome showeth the same custom to have been always amongst the old Romans: which custom of teaching youth to shoot (saith he) after it was omitted and little heed taken of, brought the whole empire of Rome to great ruin. *Schola Persica*, that is, the school of the Persians, appointed to bring up youth, whilst they were twenty year old, in shooting, is as notably known in histories as the empire of the Persians; which school, as doth appear in Cornelius Tacitus, as soon as they gave over and fell to other idle pastimes, brought both them and the Parthians under the subjection of the Romans. Plato would have common masters and stipends, for to teach youth to shoot; and, for the same purpose, he would have a broad field near every city, made common for men to use shooting in. Which saying, the more reasonably it is spoken of Plato, the more unreasonable is their deed, which would ditch up those fields privately for their own profit, which lieth open generally for the common use: men by such goods be made richer, not honester, saith Tully. If men can be persuaded to have shooting taught, this authority which followeth will persuade them, or else none, and that is, as I have once said before, of King David, whose first act and ordinance was, after he was King, that all Judea should learn to shoot. If shooting could speak, she would accuse England of unkindness and slothfulness; of unkindness toward her, because she being left to a little blind use, lacks her best maintainer, which is cunning: of slothfulness towards their own self, because they are content with that which aptness and use doth grant them in shooting, and will seek for no knowledge, as other noble commonwealths have done: and the justlier shooting might make this complaint, seeing that of fence and weapons there is made an art, a thing in no wise to be compared to shooting. For of fence, almost in every town, there is not only masters to teach it, with his provosts, ushers, scholars, and other names of art and school; but there hath not failed also, which hath diligently and favouredly* written it, and is set out in print, that every man may read it.

What discommodity doth come by the lack of knowledge, in shooting, it were over-long to rehearse. For many that have been apt, and loved shooting, because they knew not which way to hold to come to shooting, have clean turned themselves from shooting. And I may tell you, Philologe, the lack of teaching to shoot in England causeth very many men to play with the King's acts; as a man did once, either with the Mayor of London or York, I cannot tell whether, which did command by proclamation, every man in the city to hang a lantern, with a candle, afore his door; which thing the man did, but he did not light it: and so many buy bows, because of the act,* but yet they shoot not; not of evil will, but because they know not how to shoot. But, to conclude of this matter, in shooting, as in all other things, aptness is the first and chief thing; which if it be away, neither cunning nor use doth any good at all; as the Scots and Francemen, with knowledge and use of shooting, shall become good archers, when a cunning shipwright shall make a strong ship of a sallow tree; or when a husbandman shall become rich, with sowing wheat on Newmarket heath. Cunning must be had, both to set out and amend nature, and also to oversee and correct use; which use, if it be not led and governed with cunning, shall sooner go amis than straight. Use maketh perfectness in doing that thing, whereunto nature maketh a man apt, and knowledge maketh a man cunning before. So that it is not so doubtful, which of them three hath most stroke in shooting, as it is plain and evident, that all three must be had in excellent shooting.

Phi. For this communication, Toxophile, I am very glad, and that for mine own sake, because I trust now to become a shooter. And indeed I thought afore, Englishmen most apt for shooting, and I saw them daily use shooting; but yet I never found none, that would talk of any knowledge whereby a man might come to shooting. Therefore I trust that you, by the use you have had in shooting, have so thoroughly marked and noted the nature of it, that you can teach me, as it were by a trade or way, how to come to it.

Tox. I grant I have used shooting meetly well; that I might have marked it well enough, if I had been diligent. But my much shooting hath caused me study little, so that thereby I lack learning, which should set out the art or way in any thing. And you know that I was never so well seen in the *posteriorums* of Aristotle as to invent and search out general demonstrations, for the setting forth of any new science, Yet, by my troth, if you will, I will go with you into the fields at any time, and tell you as much as I can; or else you may stand some time at the pricks, and look on them which shoot best, and so learn.

Phi. How little you have looked of Aristotle, and how much learning you have lost by shooting, I cannot tell; but this I would say, and if I loved you never so ill, that you have been occupied in somewhat else beside shooting. But, to our purpose; as I will not require a trade in shooting to be taught me after the subtilty of Aristotle, even so do I not agree with you in this point, that you would have me learn to shoot with looking on them which shoot best, for so I know, I should never come to shoot meanly; for in shooting, as in all other things which be gotten by teaching, there must be showed a way, and a path, which shall lead a man to the best and chiefest point which is in shooting; which you do mark yourself well enough, and uttered it also in your communication, when you said there lay hid in the nature of shooting a certain way which, well perceived and thoroughly known, would bring a man, without any wandering, to the best end in shooting, which you called hitting of the prick. Therefore I would refer all my shooting to that end which is best, and so should I come the sooner to some mean. That which is best hath no fault, nor cannot be amended. So show me best shooting, not the best shooter; which, if he be never so good, yet hath he many a fault, easily of any man to be espied. And therefore marvel not if I require to follow that example which is without fault, rather than that which hath so many faults. And this way every wise man doth follow in teaching any manner of thing. As Aristotle, when he teacheth a man to be good, he sets not before him Socrates life, which was the best man, but chief goodness itself; according to which he would have a man direct his life.

Tox. This way which you require of me, Philologe, is too hard for me, and too high for a shooter to talk on; and taken, as I suppose, out of the midst of philosophy, to search out the perfect end of any thing; the which perfect end to find out, saith Tully, is the hardest thing in the world; the only occasion and cause why so many sects of philosophers hath been always in learning. And although, as Cicero saith, a man may imagine and dream in his mind of a perfect end in anything, yet there is no experience nor use of it, nor was never seen yet amongst men; as always to heal the sick, evermore to lead a ship without danger, at all times to hit the prick,* shall no physician, no ship-masters, no shooter ever do; and Aristotle saith that in all deeds there are two points to be marked, possibility and excellency, but chiefly a wise man must follow and lay hand on possibility, for fear he lose both. Therefore, seeing that which is most perfect and best in shooting, as always to hit the prick, was never seen nor heard tell on yet amongst men, but only imagined and thought upon in a man his mind, methink, this is the wisest counsel, and best for us to follow, rather that which a man may come to, than that which is unpossible to be attained to, lest justly that saying of the wise maid Ismene in Sophocles may be verified on us:

A fool is he that takes in hand he cannot end.

Phi. Well, if the perfect end of other matters had been as perfectly known as the perfect end of shooting is, there had never been so many sects of philosophers as there be; for in shooting both man and boy is of one opinion, that always to hit the prick is the most perfect end that can be imagined, so that we shall not need greatly contend in this matter. But now, Sir, whereas you think that a man, in learning to shoot, or any thing else, should rather wisely follow possibility, than vainly seek for perfect excellency; surely I will prove that every wise man, that wisely would learn any thing, shall chiefly go about that whereunto he knoweth well he shall never come. And you yourself, I suppose, shall confess the same to be the best way inteaching, if you will answer me to those things which I will ask of you.

Tox. And that I will gladly; both because I think it is unpossible for you to prove it, and also because I desire to hear what you can say in it.

Phi. The study of a good physician, Toxophile, I trow be to know all diseases and all medicines fit for them.

Tox. It is so indeed.*

Phi. Because, I suppose, he would gladly, at all time, heal all diseases of all men.

Tox. Yea, truly.

Phi. A good purpose surely; but was there ever physician yet among so many which hath laboured in this study, that at all times could heal all diseases?

Tox. No, truly; nor, I think, never shall be.

Phi. Then physicians, belike, study for that which none of them cometh unto. But in learning of fence, I pray you what is that which men most labour for?

Tox. That they may hit another, I trow, and never take blow their self.

Phi. You say truth, and I am sure every one of them would fain do so whensoever he playeth. But was there ever any of them so cunning yet, which, at one time or other, hath not been touched.

Tox. The best of them all is glad sometime to escape with a blow.

Phi. Then in fence also, men are taught to go about that

121

thing, which the best of them all knoweth he shall never attain unto. Moreover you that be shooters, I pray you, what mean you, when ye take so great heed to keep your standing, to shoot compass, to look on your mark so diligently, to cast up grass divers times, and other things more you know better than T. What would you do then, I pray you?

Tox. Hit the mark if we could.

Phi. And doth every man go about to hit the mark at every shot?

Tox. By my troth I trow so; and, as for myself, I am sure I do.

Phi. But all men do not hit it at all times.

which, by repeated interrogations, confutes the opponent out of his own answers.

Tox. No, truly, for that were a wonder.

Phi. Can any man hit it at all times?

Tox. No man, verily.

Phi. Then belikely, to hit the prick always is un-possible. For that is called impossible which is in no man his power to do.

Tox. Unpossible indeed.

Phi. But to shoot wide and far of the mark is a thing

possible.

Tox. No man will deny that.

Phi. But yet to hit the mark always were an excellent thing.

Tox. Excellent, surely.

Phi. Then I am sure those be wiser men which covet to shoot wide, than those which covet to hit the prick.

Tox. Why so, I pray you?

Phi. Because to shoot wide is a thing possible, and therefore, as you say yourself, of every wise man to be followed. And as for hitting the prick, because it is unpossible, it were a vain thing to go about it in good sadness,* Toxophile; thus you see that a man might go through all crafts and sciences, and prove that any man in his science coveteth that which he shall never get.

Tox. By my troth (as you say) I cannot deny but they do so; but why and wherefore they should do so, I cannot learn,

Phi. I will tell you. Every craft and science stand-eth in two things: in knowing of his craft, and working of his craft; for perfect knowledge bringeth a man to perfect working: this know painters, carvers, tailors, shoemakers, and all other craftsmen, to be true. Now, in every craft there is a perfect excellency, which may be better known in a man's mind, than followed in a man's deed. This perfectness, because it is generally laid as a broad wide example afore all men, no one particular man is able to compass it; and, as it is general to all men, so it is perpetual for all time, which proveth it a thing for man unpossible; although not for the capacity of our thinking, which is heavenly, yet, surely for the ability of our working, which is worldly. God giveth not full perfectness to one man (saith Tully) lest if one man had all in any one science, there should be nothing left for another. Yet God suffereth us to have the perfect knowledge of it, that such a knowledge, diligently followed, might bring forth, according as a man doth labour, perfect working. And who is he, that, in learning to write, would forsake an excellent example, and follow a worse? Therefore, seeing perfectness itself is an example for us, let every man study how he may come nigh it, which is a point of wisdom, not reason with God why he may not attain unto it, which is vain curiosity.

Tox. Surely this is gaily said, Philologe: but yet this one thing I am afraid of, lest this perfectness which you speak on will discourage men to take anything in hand, because, afore they begin, they know they shall never come to an end. And thus despair shall dispatch, even at the first entering it, many a good man his purpose and intent. And I think both you yourself, and all other men too, would count it mere folly for a man to tell him whom he teacheth, that he shall never obtain that which he would fainest learn. And therefore this same high and perfect way of teaching let us leave it to higher matters, and, as for shooting, it shall be content with a meaner way well enough.

Phi. Whereas you say that this high perfectness will discourage men, because they know they shall never attain unto it, Iam sure, clean contrary, there is nothing in the world shall encourage men more than it. And why ? For where a man seeth, that though another man be never so excellent, yet it is possible for himself to be better, what pain or labour will that man refuse to take? If the game be once won, no man will set forth his foot to run. And thus perfectness being so high a thing that men may look at it, not come to it, and being so plentiful and indifferent to every body, that the plentifulness of it may provoke all men to labour, because it hath enough for all men, the indifferency of it shall encourage every one to take more pain than his fellow, because every man is rewarded according to his nigh coming; and yet, which is most marvel of all, the more men take of it, the more they leave behind for other, as Socrates did in wisdom, and Cicero in eloquence, whereby other hath not lacked, but hath fared a great deal the better. And thus perfectness itself, because it is never obtained, even therefore only doth it cause so many men to be well seen and perfect in many matters as they be. But whereas you think that it were fondness to teach a man to shoot, in looking at the most perfectness in it, but rather would have a man go some other way to work; I trust no wise man will discommend that way, except he think himself wiser than Tully, which doth plainly say, that, if he teached any manner of craft, as he did rhetoric, he would labour to bring a man to the knowledge of the most perfectness of it, which knowledge should evermore lead and guide a man to do that thing well which he went about. Which way, in all manner of learning to be best, Plato doth also declare in Euthydemus, of whom Tully learned it, as he did many other things mo. And thus you see, Toxophile, by what reasons, and by whose authority I do require of you this way in teaching me to shoot; which way, I pray you, without any more delay, show me as far forth as you have noted and marked.

Tox. You call me to a thing, Philologe, which I am loth to do, and yet, if I do it not, being but a small matter as you think, you will lack friendship in me; if I take it in hand, and not bring it to pass as you would have it, you might think great want of wisdom in me.

But I advise you, seeing ye will needs have it so, the blame shall be yours, as well as mine: yours for putting upon me so instantly*; mine for receiving so fondly a greater burthen than I am able to bear. Therefore I, more willing to fulfil your mind than hoping to accomplish that which you look for, shall speak of it, not as a master of shooting, but as one not altogether ignorant in shooting. And one thing I am glad of, the sun drawing down so fast into the west shall compel me to draw apace to the end of our matter, so that his darkness shall something cloak mine ignorance.

And because you know the ordering of a matter better than

I, ask me generally of it, and I shall particularly answer to it.

Phi. Very gladly, Toxophile: for so by order those things which I would know, you shall tell the better; and those things which you shall tell, I shall remember the better.

* So *seriously.* * In order to it. * *Probably* is *speciously.* † *Faule* or *fall*, is *produce.* ‡ *Trick* or *tricksy*, is neat, nice, elegant. * *Cast* is *warped.* The word is still used by artificers. † If this line was so translated when this treatise was first written, in 1545, it is the oldest English hexameter that I remember. * *Honesty* is *honour.* † The Gnat of *Virgil,* and the Nut of *Ovid.* * Porcupine. * These lines are written in imitation of the Senarius. * *Foumards*, by others called *fumarts*, are, I believe, what we now call more commonly Stoats. * I doubt whetherour author has not mistaken the sense of chaucer: I rather take *lessing* to be *lies* than *losses* * *War* is an old word, still used in some counties for *worse;* and Ascham supposes that *war* or hostility is so named, because it is *war* or *worse* than peace. * *Atonement* is *Union,* or the act *of setting at one.* * First edition has *for.* * This paragraph is left out in the modern editions of the Toxophilus. * This parenthesis is omitted in the modern editions.† *A jack* is a coat of mail. * The word *lipe* I never saw, and know not whether I understand it: if it be the same as *leap,* it may mean a jerk or sudden motion. *Favouredly is, I suppose, *plausibly.* * The statute. * The *prick*, at other times called the *white*, is the white spot or *point* in the midst of the mark. * Here is an example of the *Socratic* method of disputation, * *Sadness* is *seriousness*, or *earnest.* First edition has "go about it: but in good sadness." * So importunately.

THE SECOND BOOK OF THE SCHOOL OF SHOOTING

Philologus.   Toxophilus.

Phi. WHAT is the chief point in shooting, that every man laboureth to come to?

Tox. To hit the mark.

Phi. How many things are required to make a man evermore hit the mark?

Tox. Two.

Phi. Which two?

Tox. Shooting straight, and keeping of a length.

Phi. How should a man shoot straight, and how should a man keep a length?

Tox. In knowing and having things belonging to shooting; and when they be known and had, in well handling of them; whereof some belong to shooting straight, some to keeping of a length, some commonly to them both, as shall be told severally of them in place convenient.

Phi. Things belonging to shooting, which be they?

Tox. All things be outward *; and some be instruments for every sere archer to bring with him, proper for his own use : other things be general to every man, as the place and time serveth.

Phi. Which be instruments?

Tox. Bracer, shooting glove, string, bow, and shaft.

Phi. Which be general to all men?

Tox. The weather and the mark; yet the mark is ever under the rule of the weather.

Phi. Wherein standeth well handling of things?

Tox. Altogether within a man himself: some handling is proper to instruments, some to the weather, some to the mark, some is within a man himself.

Phi. What handling is proper to the instruments?

Tox. Standing, knocking, drawing, holding, loosing, whereby cometh fair shooting, which neither belong to wind nor weather, nor yet to the mark; for in a rain and at no mark, a man may shoot a fair shoot.

Phi. Well said: what handling belongeth to the weather?

Tox. Knowing of his wind, with him, against him, side wind, full side wind, side wind quarter with him, side wind quarter against him, and so forth.

Phi. Well then, go to; what handling belongeth to the mark?

Tox. To mark his standing, to shoot compass, to draw evermore like, to loose evermore like, to consider the nature of the prick, in hills and dales, in straight plains and winding places, and also to espy his mark.

Phi. Very well done. And what is only within a man himself?

Tox. Good heed-giving, and avoiding all affections : which things oftentimes do mar and make all. And these things spoken of me generally and briefly, if they be well known, had, and handled, shall bring a man to such shooting, as few or none ever yet came unto; but surely if he miss in any one of them, he can never hit the mark; and in the more he doth miss, the farther he shooteth from his mark. But, as in all other matters, the first step or stair to be good, is to know a man's fault, and then to amend it; and he that will not know his fault, shall never amend it.

Phi. You speak now, Toxophile, even as I would have you to speak; but let us return again unto our matter, and those things which you have packed up in so short a room, we will loose them forth, and take every piece, as it were, in our hand, and look more narrowly upon it.

Tox. I am content; but we will rid them as fast as we can, because the sun goeth so fast down, and yet somewhat must needs be said of every one of them.

Phi. Well said; and I trow we began with those things

which be instruments, whereof the first, as I suppose, was the bracer.

Tox. Little is to be said of the bracer. A bracer* serveth for two causes, one to save his arm from the stripe of the string, and his doublet from wearing; and the other is, that the string gliding sharply and quickly off the bracer, may make the sharper shot. For if the string should light upon the bare sleeve, the strength of the shoot should stop and die there. But it is best, by my judgement, to give the bow so much bent, that the string need never touch a man's arm, and so should a man need no bracer, as I know many good archers which occupy none. In a bracer a man must take heed of three things; that it have no nails in it, that it have no buckles, that it be fast on with laces without agglets. For the nails will sheer in sunder a man's string before he be ware, and so put his bow in jeopardy: buckles and agglets at unwares shall raze his bow, a thing both evil for the sight, and perilous for fretting. And thus a bracer is only had for this purpose, that the string may have ready passage.

Phi. In my bracer I am cunning enough; but what say you of the shooting glove?

Tox. A shooting glove is chiefly for to save a man's fingers from hurting, that he may be able to bear the sharp string to the uttermost of his strength. And when a man shooteth, the might of his shoot lieth on the foremost finger, and on the ringman; for the middle finger which is the longest, like a lubber, starteth back, and beareth no weight of the string in a manner at all; therefore the two other fingers must have thicker leather, and that must have thickest of all whereon a man looseth most, and for sure loosing, the foremost finger is most apt, because it holdeth best; and for that purpose, nature hath, as a man would say, yoked it with the thumb. Leather, if it be next a man's skin, will sweat, wax hard, and chafe; therefore scarlet, for the softness of it and thickness withal, is good to sew within a man's glove. If that will not serve, but yet your finger hurteth, you must take a searing cloth, made of fine virgin wax and deers' suet, and put next your finger, and so on with your glove. If yet you feel your finger pinched, leave shooting, both because then you shall shoot naught; and again by little and little, hurting your finger, ye shall make it long and long too or you shoot again. A new glove plucks many shoots, because the string goeth not freely off; and therefore the fingers must be cut short and trimmed with some ointment, that the string may glide well away. Some with holding in the nock of their shaft too hard, rub the skin off their fingers. For this there be two remedies, one to have a goose quill splitted and sewed against the nocking, betwixt the lining and the leather, which shall help the shoot much too; the other way is to have some roll of leather sewed betwixt his fingers, at the setting on of the fingers, which shall keep his fingers so in sunder that they shall not hold the nock so fast as they did. The shooting glove hath a purse, which shall serve to put fine linen cloth and wax in, two necessary things for a shooter. Some men use gloves or other such like thing on their bow-hand for chafing, because they hold so hard. But that cometh commonly when a bow is not round, but somewhat square; fine wax shall do very well in such a case to lay where a man holdeth his bow; and thus much as concerning your glove.

And these things, although they be trifles, yet because you be but a young shooter, I would not leave them out.

Phi. And so you shall do me most pleasure. The string I trow be the next.

Tox. The next indeed; a thing, though it be little, yet not a little to be regarded. But herein you must be content to put your trust in honest stringers. And surely stringers ought more diligently to be looked upon by the officers, than either bowyer or fletcher, because they may deceive a simple man the more easilier. An ill string breaketh many a good bow, nor no other thing half so many. In war, if a string break, the man is lost, and is no man, for his weapon is gone; and although he have two strings put on at once, yet he shall have small leisure and less room to bend his bow; therefore God send us good stringers both for war and peace. Now what a string ought to be made on, whether of good hemp, as they do now-a-days, or of flax, or of silk, I leave that to the judgement of stringers, of whom we must buy them. Eustathius, upon this verse of Homer,

Twang quoth the bow, and twang quoth the string, out quickly
the shaft flew,*

*doth tell, that in old time, they made their bow-strings of
bullocks' thermes,† which they twined together as they do ropes;
and therefore they made a great twang. Bow-strings also hath
been made of the hair of an horse tail, called, for the matter
of them, Hippias, as doth appear in many good authors of
the Greek tongue. Great strings and little strings be for divers
purposes : the great string is more surer for the bow, more stable
to prick withall, but slower for the cast. The little string is clean
contrary, not so sure, therefore to be taken heed of, lest with
long tarrying on it break your bow, more fit to shoot far, than
apt to prick near; therefore, when you know the nature of both
big and little, you must fit your bow according to the occasion
of your shooting. In stringing of your bow (though this place
belong rather to the handling than to the thing itself, yet because
the thing, and the handling of the thing, be so joined together,
I must need sometimes couple the one with the other) you must
mark the fit length of your bow. For, if the string be too short,
the bending will give, and at the last slip, and so put the bow
in jeopardy. If it be long, the bending must needs be in the
small of the string, which being sore twined, must needs snap
in sunder, to the destruction of many good bows. Moreover, you
must look that your bow be well nocked, for fear the sharpness of
the horn sheer asunder the string. And that chanceth oft when*

in bending, the string hath but one wap to strengthen it withal. You must mark also to set your string straight on, or else the one end shall writhe contrary to the other, and so break your bow. When the string beginneth never so little to wear, trust it not, but away with it; for it is an ill saved halfpenny, that costs a man a crown. Thus you see how many jeopardies hangeth over the silly poor bow, by reason only of the string. As when the string is short, when it is long, when either of the nocks be naught, when it hath but one wap, and when it tarrieth over long on.

Phi. I see well it is no marvel, though so many bows be broken.

Tox. Bows be broken twice as many ways beside these. But again, in stringing your bow, you must look for much bend or little bend, for they be clean contrary. The little bend hath but one commodity, which is in shooting faster, and farther shoot, and the cause thereof is, because the string hath so far a passage or it part with the shaft. The great bend hath many commodities; for it maketh easier shooting, the bow being half drawn before. It needeth no bracer, for the string stoppeth before it come at the arm. It will not so soon hit a man's sleeve or other gear, by the same reason. It hurteth not the shaft feather, as the low bend doth. It suffereth a man better to espy his mark. Therefore let your bow have good big bend, a shaftment and two fingers at the least, for these which I have spoken of.

Phi. The bracer, glove, and string, be done; now you must come to the bow, the chief instrument of all.

Tox. Divers countries and times have used always divers bows, and of divers fashions. Horn bows are used in some places now, and were used also in Homer's days; for Pandarus bow, the best shooter among all the Trojans, was made of two goat horns joined together ; the length whereof, saith Homer, was sixteen hand-breadths, not far differing from the length of our bows. Scripture maketh mention of brass bows. Iron bows, and steel bows, have been of long time, and also now are used among the Turks; but yet they must needs be unprofitable. For if brass, iron, or steel, have their own strength and pith in them, they be far above man's strength: if they be made meet for man's strength, their pith is nothing worth to shoot any shoot withal. The Ethiopians had bows of palm-tree, which seemed to be very strong; but we have none experience of them. The length of them was four cubits. The men of Inde had their bows made of a reed, which was of a great strength. And no marvel though bow and shafts were made thereof; for the reeds be so great in Inde, as Herodotus saith, that of every joint of a reed a man may make a fisher's boat. These bows, saith Arrianus in Alexander's life, gave so great a stroke, that no harness or buckler, though it were never so strong, could withstand it. The length of such a bow was even with the length of him that used it. The Lycians used bows made of a tree, called in Latin *Cornus* (as concerning the name of it in

English, I can sooner prove that other men call it false, than I can tell the right name of it myself,) this wood is as hard as horn, and very fit for shafts, as shall be told after. Ovid showeth that Syringa the nymph, and one of the maidens of Diana, had a bow of this wood, whereby the poet meaneth, that it was very excellent to make bows of.

As for Brazil, elm, wych, and ash, experience doth prove them to be but mean for bows ; and so to conclude, yew, of all other things, is that whereof perfect shooting would have a bow made. This wood as it is now general and common amongst Englishmen, so hath it continued from long time, and had in most price for bows, amongst the Romans, as doth appear in this half verse of Virgil:

Taxi torquentur in arcus.
Yew fit for a bow to be made on.

Now, as I say, a bow of yew must be had for perfect shooting at the pricks; which mark, because it is certain, and most certain rules may be given of it, shall serve for our communication at this time. A good bow is known, much-what as good counsel is known, by the end and proof of it; and yet both a bow and good counsel may be made both better and worse, by well or ill handling of them, as oftentimes chanceth. And as a man both must and will take counsel of a wise and honest man, though he see not the end of it; so must a shooter, of necessity, trust an honest and good bowyer for a bow, afore he know the proof of it. And as a wise man will take plenty of counsel afore-hand, whatsoever need, so a shooter should have always three or four bows in store, whatsoever chance.

Phi. But if I trust bowyers always, sometime I am like to be deceived.

Tox. Therefore shall I tell you some tokens in a bow, that you shall be the seldomer deceived. If you come into a shop, and find a bow that is small, long, heavy, and strong, lying straight, not winding, not marred with knot gall, wind-shake, wem, fret or pinch, buy that bow of my warrant. The best colour of a bow that I find, is when the back and the belly in working be much-what after one manner, for such oftentimes in wearing do prove like virgin wax or gold, having a fine long grain, even from the one end of the bow to the other; the short grain, although such prove well sometime, are for the most part very brittle. Of the making of the bow, I will not greatly meddle, lest I should seem to enter into another man's occupation, which I can no skill of. Yet I would desire all bowyers to season their staves well, to work them and sink them well, to give them heats convenient, and tillerings* plenty. For thereby they should both get themselves a good name, (and a good name increaseth a man's profit much,) and also do great commodity to the whole realm. If any men do offend in this point, I am afraid they be those journeymen, which labour more speedily to make many bows for their money sake, than they work diligently to make good bows for the commonwealth sake, not laying before their eyes this wise proverb, "Soon enough, if well enough;" wherewith every honest handy-craftsmen should measure, as it were with a rule, his work withal. He that is a journeyman, and rideth upon another man's horse, if he ride an honest pace, no man will disallow him; but if he make post haste, both he that owneth the horse, and he peradventure also that afterward shall buy the horse, may chance to curse him. Such hastiness, I am afraid, may also be found amongst some of them which, throughout the realm, in divers places, work the King's artillery for war; thinking, if they get a bow or a sheaf of arrows to some fashion, they be good enough for bearing gear. And thus that weapon, which is the chief defence of the realm, very oft doth little service to him that should use it, because it is so negligently wrought of him that should make it; when truly I suppose that neither the bow can be too good and chief wood, nor yet too well seasoned or truly made, with heatings and tillerings, neither that shaft too good wood, or too thoroughly wrought, with the best pinion feathers that can be gotten; wherewith a man shall serve his Prince, defend his country, and save himself. from his enemy. And I trust no man will be angry with me for speaking thus, but those which find themselves touched therein : which ought rather to be angry with themself for doing so, than to be miscontent with me for saying so. And in no case they ought to be displeased with me, seeing this is spoken also after that sort, not for the noting of any person severally, but for the amending of every one generally.

But turn we again to know a good shooting bow for our purpose. Every bow is made either of a bough, of a plant, or of the bole of the tree. The bough commonly is very knotty, and full of pins, weak, of small pith, and soon will follow the string, and seldom wear-eth to any fair colour; yet for children and young beginners it may serve well enough. The plant proveth many times well, if it be of a good and clean growth; and, for the pith of it, is quick enough of cast, it will ply and bow far afore it break, as all other young things do. The bole of the tree is cleanest without knot or pin, having a fast and hard wood, by reason of his full growth, strong and mighty of cast, and best for a bow, if the staves be even cloven, and be afterwards wrought, not overthwart the wood, but as the grain and straight growing of the wood leadeth a man; or else, by all reason, it must soon break, and that in many shivers. This must be considered in the rough wood, and when the bow staves be over-wrought and fashioned. For in dressing and piking it up for a bow, it is too late to look for it.

But yet in these points, as I said before, you must trust an honest bowyer, to put a good bow in your hand, somewhat looking yourself to those tokens I showed you. And you must not stick for a groat or twelvepence more than another man would give, if it be a good bow. For a good bow twice paid for, is better than an ill bow once broken.

Thus a shooter must begin, not at the making of his bow, like a bowyer, but at the buying of his bow, like an archer. And, when his bow is bought and brought home, afore he trust much upon it, let him try and trim it after this sort.

Take your bow into the field, shoot in him, sink him with dead heavy shafts, look where he cometh most, provide for that place betimes, lest it pinch, and so fret: when you have thus shot in him, and perceived good shooting wood in him, you must have him again to a good, cunning, and trusty workman, which shall cut him shorter, and pike him and dress him fitter, make him come round compass everywhere, and whipping at the ends, but with discretion, lest he whip in sunder, or else fret, sooner than he is ware of: he must also lay him straight, if he be cast, or otherwise need require; and if he be flat made, gather him round, and so shall he both shoot the faster for far shooting, and also the surer for near pricking.

Phi. What if I come into a shop, and spy out a bow, which shall both then please me very well when I buy him, and be also very fit and meet for me when I shoot in him; so that he be both weak enough for easy shooting, also quick and speedy enough for far casting; then, I would think, I shall need no more business with him, but be content with him, and use him well enough, and so, by that means, avoid both great trouble, and also some cost, which you cunning archers very often put yourselves unto, being very Englishmen, never ceasing piddling about your bow and shafts, when they be well, but either with shorting and piking your bows, or else with new feathering, piecing and heading your shafts, can never have done until they be stark naught.

Tox. Well, Philologe, surely if I have any judgment at all in shooting, it is no very great good token in a bow, whereof nothing when it is new and fresh need be cut away; even as Cicero saith of a young man's wit and style, which you know better than I. For every new thing must always have more than it needeth, or else it will not wax better and better, but ever decay, and be worse and worse. New ale, if it run not over the barrel when it is new tunned, will soon lease [*lose*] his pith* and his head afore he be long drawn on. And likewise as that colt, which, at the first taking up, needeth little breaking and handling, but is fit and gentle enough for the saddle, seldom or never proveth well: even so that bow, which at the first buying, without any more proof and trimming, is fit and easy to shoot in, shall neither be profitable to last long, nor yet pleasant to shoot well. And therefore as a young horse full of courage, with handling and breaking is brought unto a sure pace and going, so shall a new bow, fresh and quick of cast, by sinking and cutting be brought to a stedfast shooting. And an easy and gentle bow, when it is new, is not much unlike a soft-spirited boy, when he is young. But yet, as of an unruly boy with right handling, proveth oftenest of all a well-ordered man; so of an unfit and staffish bow, with good trimming, must needs follow always a stedfast shooting bow. And, such a perfect bow, which never will deceive a man, except a man deceive it, must be had for that perfect end which you look for in shooting.

Phi. Well, Toxophile, I see well you be cunninger in this gear than I; but put case that I have three or four such good bows, piked and dressed as you now speak of, yet I do remember that many learned men do say, that it is easier to get a good thing, than to save and keep a good thing; wherefore, if you can teach me as concerning that point, you have satisfied me plentifully as concerning a bow.

Tox. Truly it was the next thing that I would have come unto, for so the matter lay. When you have brought your bow to such a point as I speak of, then you must have an herden or woollen cloth waxed, wherewith every day you must rub and chafe your bow, till it shine and glitter withal: which thing shall cause it both to be clean, well favoured, goodly of colour, and shall also bring, as it were, a crust over it, that is to say, shall make it every where on the outside so slippery and hard, that neither any wet or weather can enter to hurt it, nor yet any fret, or pinch, be able to bite upon it; but that you shall do it great wrong before you break it. This must be done oftentimes, but especially when you come from shooting.

Beware also when you shoot off your shaft heads, dagger, knives, or agglets, lest they rase your bow; a thing, as I said before, both unseemly to look on, and also dangerous for frets. Take heed also of misty and dankish days, which shall hurt a bow more than any rain. For then you must either always rub it, or else leave shooting.

Your bow-case (this I did not promise to speak of, because it is without the nature of shooting, or else I should trouble me with other things infinite more : yet seeing it is a safeguard for the bow, something I will say of it) your bow-case, I say, if you ride forth, must neither be too wide for your bows, for so shall one clap upon another, and hurt them, nor yet so strait that scarce they can be thrust in, for that would lay them on side, and wind them. A bow case of leather is not the best; for that is oft-times moist, which hurteth the bows very much.

Therefore I have seen good shooters which would have for every bow a sere case, made of woollen cloth, and then you may put three or four of them, so cased, into a leather case if you will. This woollen case shall both keep them in sunder, and also will keep a bow in his full strength, that it never give for any weather.

At home these wood * cases be very good for bows to stand in. But take heed that your bow stand not too near a stone wall, for that will make him moist and weak, nor yet too near any fire, for that will make him short and brittle. And thus much as concerning the saving and keeping of your bow; now you shall hear what things you must avoid, for fear of breaking your bow.

A shooter chanceth to break his bow commonly four ways;

by the string, by the shaft, by drawing too far, and by frets. By the string, as I said before, when the string is either too short, too long, not surely put on, with one wap, or put crooked on, or shorn in sunder with an evil nock, or suffered to tarry overlong on. When the string fails the bow must needs break, and especially in the middle; because both the ends have nothing to stop them; but whips so far back, that the belly must needs violently rise up, the which you shall well perceive in bending of a bow backward. Therefore a bow that followeth the string is least hurt with breaking of strings.

By the shaft a bow is broken, either when it is too short, and so you set it in your bow, or when the nock breaks for littleness, or when the string slips without the nock for wideness, then you pull it to your ear and lets it go, which must needs break the shaft at the least, and put string and bow and all in jeopardy, because the strength of the bow hath nothing in it to stop the violence of it. This kind of breaking is most perilous for the standers-by, for in such a case you shall see some time the end of a bow fly a whole score from a man, and that most commonly, as I have marked oft, the upper end of the bow.

The bow is drawn too far two ways. Either when you take a longer shaft than your own, or else when you shift your hand too low or too high for shooting far. This way pulleth the back in sunder, and then the bow flieth in many pieces.

So when you see a bow broken, having the belly risen up

both ways or tone, the string brake it. When it is broken in two pieces, in a manner even off, and specially in the upper end, the shaft nock brake it. When the back is pulled asunder in many pieces, too far drawing brake it. These tokens either always be true, or else very seldom miss.

The fourth thing that breaketh a bow is frets, which make a bow ready and apt to break by any of the three ways aforesaid. Frets be in a shaft as well as in a bow, and they be much like a canker, creeping and increasing in those places in a bow, which be weaker than other. And for this purpose must your bow be well trimmed and piked of a cunning man, that it may come round in true compass every where. For frets you must beware if your bow have a knot in the back, lest the places which be next it be not allowed strong enough to bear with the knot, or else the strong knot shall fret the weak places next it. Frets be first little pinches, the which when you perceive, pike the places about the pinches, to make them somewhat weaker, and as well coming as where it pinched, and so the pinches shall die, and never increase further into great frets.

Frets begin many times in a pin, for there the good wood is corrupted, that it must needs be weak; and because it is weak, therefore it frets. Good bowyers therefore do raise every pin, and allow it more wood for fear of fretting.

Again, bows most commonly fret under the hand, not so much as some men suppose for the moistness of the hand, as for the heat of the hand. The nature of heat, saith Aristotle, is to loose, and not to knit fast, and the more looser the more weaker, the more weaker the readier to fret.

A bow is not well made which hath not wood plenty in the hand. For if the ends of the bow be staffish, or a man's hand any thing hot, the belly must needs soon fret. Remedy for frets to any purpose I never heard tell of any, but only to make the fretted place as strong, or stronger, than any other. To fill up the fret with little shivers of a quill and glue, as some say will do well, by reason must be stark nought. For, put case the fret did cease then; yet the cause which made it fret afore, (and that is weakness of the place,) because it is not taken away, must needs make it fret again. As for cutting out of frets, with all manner of piecing of bows, I will clean exclude from perfect shooting. For pieced bows be much like old housen, which be more chargeable to repair than commodious to dwell in. And again, to swaddle a bow much about with bands, very seldom doth any good, except it be to keep down a spell in the back, otherwise. bands either need not, when the bow is anything worth, or else boot not, when it is marred and past best. And although I know mean and poor shooters will use pieced and banded bows sometime, because they are not able to get better when they would; yet, I am sure, if they consider it well, they shall find it both less charge and more pleasure, to bestowe* at any time a couple of shillings of a new bow, than to bestow ten pence of piecing an old bow. For better is cost upon somewhat worth, than spence [*expence*] upon nothing worth. And this I speak also, because you would have me refer all to perfectness in shooting.

Moreover, there is another thing, which will soon cause a bow to be broken by one of the three ways which be first spoken of; and that is shooting in winter,† when there is any frost. Frost is wheresoever is any waterish humour, as is in all woods, either more or less; and you know that all things frozen and icy will rather break than bend. Yet, if a man must needs shoot at any such time, let him take his bow and bring it to the fire; and there, by little and little, rub and chafe it with a waxed cloth, which shall bring it to that point that he may shoot safely enough in it. This rubbing with wax, as I said before, is a great succour against all wet and moistness. In the fields also, in going betwixt the pricks, either with your hand, or else with a cloth, you must keep your bow in such a temper.

And thus much as concerning your bow, how first to know what wood is best for a bow, then to choose a bow, after to trim a bow, again to keep it in goodness; last of all, how to save it from all harm and evilness. And although many men can say more of a bow, yet I trust these things be true, and almost sufficient for the knowledge of a perfect bow.

Phi. Surely I believe so, and yet I could have heard you talk longer on it; although I cannot see what may be said more of it. Therefore, except you will pause a while, you may go forward to a shaft.

Tox. What shafts were made of in old time, authors do not so manifestly show, as of bows. Herodotus doth tell, that in the flood of Nilus there was a beast, called a Water Horse, of whose skin, after it was dried, the Egyptians made shafts and darts on. The tree called Cornus was so common to make shafts of, that, in good authors of the Latin tongue, Cornus is taken for a shaft, as in Seneca, and that place of Virgil,

Volat Itala cornus.

Yet, of all things that ever I marked of old authors, either Greek or Latin, for shafts to be made of, there is nothing so common as reeds. Herodotus, in describing the mighty host of Xerxes, doth tell, that three great countries used shafts made of a reed; the Ethiopians, the Lycians (whose shafts lacked feathers, whereat I marvel most of all), and the men of Inde. The shafts in Inde were very long, a yard and an half, as Arrianus doth say; or at the least a yard, as Q. Curtius doth say, and therefore they gave the greater stripe; but yet, because they were so long, they were the more unhandsome, and less profitable to men of Inde, as Curtius doth tell.

In Crete and Italy they used to have their shafts of reed also. The best reed for shafts grew in Inde, and in Rhenus, a flood of Italy. But, because such shafts be neither easy for Englishmen to get, and, if they were gotten, scarce profitable for them to use, I will let them pass, and speak of those shafts which Englishmen, at this day, most commonly do approve and allow. A shaft hath three principal parts, the stele, the feathers, and the head; whereof every one must be severally spoken of.

Steles be made of divers woods : as,

Brazil,	Service-tree,
Turkey wood,	Hulder [*Alder*],
Fustic,	Blackthorn,
Sugar-chest,	Beech,
Hardbeam,	Elder,
Birch,	Asp,
Ash,	Sallow.
Oak,	

These woods, as they be most commonly used, so they be most fit to be used : yet some one fitter than another for divers men's shooting, as shall be told afterward. And in this point, as in a bow, you must trust an honest fletcher. Nevertheless, although I cannot teach you to make a bow or a shaft, which belongeth to a bowyer and a fletcher to come to their living, yet will I show you some tokens to know a bow and a shaft, which pertaineth to an archer to come to good shooting.

A stele must be well seasoned for casting,* and it must be made as the grain lieth, and as it groweth, or else it will never fly clean, as cloth cut overthwart, and against the wool, can never hose a man clean. A knotty stele may be suffered in a big shaft, but for a little shaft it is nothing fit, both because it will never fly far ; and, besides that it is ever in danger of breaking, it flyeth not far because the strength of the shoot is hindered and stopped at the knot, even as a stone cast into a plain even still water, will make the water move a great space ; yet, if there be any whirling plat in the water, the moving ceaseth when it cometh at the whirling plat, which is not much unlike a knot in a shaft, if it be considered well. So everything as it is plain and straight of his own nature, so is it fittest for far moving. Therefore a stele which is hard to stand in a bow without knot, and straight, (I mean not artificially straight as the fletcher doth make it, but naturally straight as it groweth in the wood,) is best to make a shaft of, either to go clean, fly far, or stand surely in any weather.

Now how big, how small, how heavy, how light, how long, how short, a shaft should be particularly for every man, seeing we must talk of the general nature of shooting, cannot be told; no more than you rhetoricians can appoint any one kind of words, of sentences, of figures, fit for every matter; but even as the man and the matter requireth, so the fittest to be used. Therefore as concerning those contraries in a shaft, every man must avoid them, and draw to the mean of them, which mean is best in all things. Yet if a man happen to offend in any of the extremes, it is better to offend in want and scantness, than in too much and outrageous exceeding. As it is better to have a shaft a little too short than over-long, somewhat too light than over-lumpish, a little too small than a great deal too big; which thing is not only truly said in shooting, but in all other things that ever man goeth about; as in eating, talking, and all other things like; which matter was once excellently disputed upon in the schools, you know when.

And to offend in these contraries, cometh much, if men take not heed, through the kind of wood whereof the shaft is made; for some wood belongs to the exceeding part, some to the scant part, some to the mean, as Brazil, Turkey wood, fustic, sugar-chest, and such like, make dead, heavy, lumpish, hobbling shafts. Again, alder, blackthorn, service tree, beech, elder, asp, and sallow, either for their weakness or lightness, make hollow, starting, studding, gadding shafts. But birch, hardbeam, some oak, and some ash, being both strong enough to stand in a bow, and also light enough to fly far, are best for a mean, which is to be sought out in every thing. And although I know that some men shoot so strong, that the dead woods be light enough for them, and other some so weak, that the loose woods be likewise for them big enough, yet generally, for the most part of men, the mean is the best. And so to conclude, that is always best for a man which is meetest for him. Thus no wood of his own nature is either too light or too heavy, but as the shooter is himself which doth use it. For that shaft, which one year for a man is too light and scudding, for the self-same man the next year may chance to be heavy and hobbling. Therefore cannot I express, except generally, which is best wood for a shaft; but let every man, when he knoweth his own strength, and the nature of every wood, provide and fit himself thereafter. Yet, as concerning sheaf arrows for war, (as I suppose) it were better to make them of good ash, and not of asp, as they be now-a-days. For of all other woods that ever I proved, ash being big is swiftest, and again heavy to give a great stripe withal, which asp shall not do. What heaviness doth in a stripe, every man by experience can tell; therefore ash being both swifter * and heavier, is more fit for sheaf arrows than asp : And thus much for the best wood for shafts.

Again, likewise, as no one wood can be greatly meet for all kinds of shafts, no more can one fashion of the stele be fit for every shooter. For those that be little-breasted and big toward the head, called, by their likeness, taper fashion, resh grown, and of some merry fellows bobtails, be fit for them which shoot under-hand, because they shoot with a soft loose, and stresses not a shaft much in the breast, where the weight of the bow lieth, as you may perceive by the wearing of every shaft. Again, the big-breasted shaft is fit for him which shooteth right afore him, or else the breast being weak, should never withstand that strong pithy kind of shooting: thus, the under-hand must have a small breast to go clean away out of the bow, the fore hand must have a big breast to bear the great might of the bow. The shaft must be made round, nothing flat, without gall or wem, for this purpose. For because roundness (whether you take example in heaven or in earth) is fittest shape and form both for fast moving, and also for soon piercing of any thing. And therefore Aristotle saith, that nature hath made the rain to be round, because it should the easilier enter through the air.

The nock of the shaft is diversely made; for some be great and full, some handsome and little; some wide, some narrow, some deep, some shallow, some round, some long, some with

one nock, some with a double nock, whereof every one hath
his property. The great and full nock may be well felt, and
many ways they save a shaft from breaking. The handsome
and little nock will go clean away from the hand; the wide
nock is naught, both for breaking of the shaft and also for
sudden slipping out of the string, when the narrow nock doth
avoid both those harms. The deep and long nock is good in
war for sure keeping in of the string. The shallow and round
nock is best for our purpose in pricking for clean deliverance
of a shoot. And double nocking is used for double surety of
the shaft. And thus far as concerning a whole stele. Piecing
of a shaft with Brazil and holly, or other heavy woods, is to
make the end compass heavy * with the feathers in flying for
the stedfaster shooting. For if the end were plump heavy with
lead, and the wood next it light, the head end would ever be
downwards, and never fly straight. Two points in piecing be
enough, lest the moistness of the earth enter too much into
the piecing, and so loose the glue. Therefore many points be
more pleasant to the eye, than profitable for the use. Some
use to piece their shafts in the nock with Brazil or holly, to
counterweigh, with the head; and I have seen some for the
same purpose bore a hole a little beneath the nock, and put
lead in it. But yet none of these ways be any thing needful
at all: for the nature of a feather in flying, if a man mark it
well, is able to bear up a wonderful weight; and I think such
piecing came up first thus: when a good archer hath broken a

good shaft in the feathers, and for the fantasy he hath had to it, he is loth to lose it, and therefore doth he piece it. And then by and by, other, either because it is gay, or else because they will have a shaft like a good archer, cutteth their whole shafts, and pieceth them again; a thing, by my judgment, more costly than needful. And thus have you heard what wood, what fashion, what nocking, what piecing, a stele must have. Now followeth the feathering.

Phi. I would never have thought you could have said half so much of a stele; and, I think as concerning the little feather, and the plain head, there is but little to say.

Tox. Little! yes, truly: for there is no one thing in all shooting so much to be looked on as the feather. For, first, a question may be asked: Whether any other thing beside a feather, be fit for a shaft or no? If a feather only be fit, whether a goose feather only or no? If a goose feather be best, then whether there be any difference as concerning the feather of an old goose and a young goose; a gander or a goose; a fenny goose or an uplandish goose? Again, which is best feather in any goose, the right wing or the left wing; the pinion feather or any other feather: a white, black, or grey feather; Thirdly, in setting on of your feather, whether it is pared or drawn with a thick rib or a thin rib, (the rib is the hard quill which divideth the feather,) a long feather better or a short, set on near the nock or far from the nock, set on straight or somewhat bowing; and whether one or two feathers run on the bow? Fourthly, in couling or sheering, whether high or low, whether somewhat swine-backed (I must use shooters' words) or saddle-backed, whether round or square shorn? And whether a shaft at any time ought to be plucked, and how to be plucked?

Phi. Surely, Toxophile, I think many fletchers, although daily they have these things in use, if they were asked suddenly, what they would say of a feather, they could not say so much. But I pray you let me hear you more at large express those things in a feather, the which you packed up in so narrow a room. And first, whether any other thing may be used for a feather or not?

Tox. That was the first point indeed; and because there followeth many after, I will hie apace over them, as one that had many a mile to ride. Shafts to have had always feathers, Pliny in Latin, and Julius Pollux in Greek, do plainly show; yet only the Lycians I read in Herodotus to have used shafts without feathers. Only a feather is fit for a shaft for two causes; first because it is leath,* weak to give place to the bow, then because it is of that nature that it will start up after the bow. So plate, wood, or horn, cannot serve, because they will not give place. Again, cloth, paper, or parchment, cannot serve, because they will not rise after the bow; therefore a feather is only meet, because it only will do both. Now, to look on the feathers of all manner of birds, you shall see some so low, weak, and short, some so coarse, stoore, and hard, and the rib so brickle, thin and narrow, that it can neither be drawn,

157

pared, nor yet will set on; that except it be a swan for a dead shaft, (as I know some good archers have used,) or a duck for a flight, which lasts but one shot, there is no feather but only of a goose that hath all commodities in it. And truly at a short butt, which some men doth use, the peacock feather doth seldom keep up the shaft either right or level, it is so rough and heavy; so that many men, which have taken them up for gayness, hath laid them down again for profit: thus, for our purpose, the goose is the best feather for the best shooter.

Phi. No, that is not so; for the best shooter that ever was, used other feathers.

Tox. Yea, are you so cunning in shooting? I pray you who was that?

Phi. Hercules, which had his shafts feathered with eagles' feathers, as Hesiodus doth say.

Tox. Well, as for Hercules, seeing neither water nor land, heaven nor hell, could scarce content him to abide in, it was no marvel though a silly poor goose-feather could not please him to shoot withal; and again, as for eagles, they fly so high, and build so far off, that they be very hard to come by. Yet, well fare the gentle goose, which bringeth to a man, even to his door, so many exceeding commodities. For the goose is man's comfort in war and in peace, sleeping and waking. What praise soever is given to shooting, the goose may challenge the best part in it. How well doth she make a man fare at his table? How easily doth she make a man lie in his bed? How fit even as her feathers be only for shooting, so be her quills fit only for writing.

Phi. Indeed, Toxophile, that is the best praise you gave to a goose yet; and surely I would have said you had been to blame, if you had overskipt it.

Tox. The Romans, I trow, Philologe, not so much because a goose with crying saved their capitol, and head tower, with their golden Jupiter, as Propertius doth say very prettily in this verse,

Anseris et tutum voce fuisse Jovem, Id est,

Thieves on a night had stolen Jupiter, had a goose not a

kekede [*cackled*],

did make a golden goose, and set her in the top of the capitolium, and appointed also the censors to allow out of the common hutch yearly stipends, for the finding of certain geese;—the Romans did not, I say, give all this honour to a goose for that good deed only, but for other infinite mo, which come daily to a man by geese; and surely if I should declaim in the praise of any manner of best living, I would choose a goose. But the goose hath made us flee too far from our matter. Now, Sir, ye have heard how a feather must be had, and that a goose feather only; it followeth of a young goose and an old, and the residue belonging to a feather; which thing I will shortly course over; whereof, when you know the properties, you may fit your shafts according to your shooting, which rule you must observe in all other things too, because no one fashion or quantity can be fit for every man, no more than a shoe or a coat can be. The old goose feather is stiff and strong, good for a wind, and fittest for a dead shaft: the young goose feather is weak and fine, best for a swift shaft; and it must be couled at the first sheering, somewhat high, for with shooting it will settle and fall very much. The same thing (although not so much) is to be considered in a goose and a gander. A fenny goose, even as her flesh is blacker, stoorer, unwholsomer, so is her feather, for the same cause, coarser, stoorer, and rougher; and therefore I have heard very good fletchers say, that the second feather in some place is better than the pinion in other some. Betwixt the wings is little difference, but that you must have divers shafts of one flight, feathered with divers wings, for divers winds; for if the wind and the feather go both one way, the shaft will be carried too much. The pinion feathers, as it hath the first place in the wing, so it hath the first place in good feathering. You may know it before it be pared, by a bought which is in it; and again when it is cold, by the thinness above, and the thickness at the ground; and also by the stiffness and fineness which will carry a shaft better, faster, and further, even as a fine sail-cloth doth a ship.

The colour of the feather is least to be regarded, yet somewhat to be looked on; for a good white you have sometime an ill grey. Yet, surely it standeth with good reason, to have the cock-feather black or grey, as it were to give a man warning to nock right. The cock-feather is called that which standeth above in right nocking; which if you do not observe, the other feathers must needs run on the bow, and so marr your shot. And thus far of the goodness and choice of your feather: now folioweth the setting on. Wherein you must look that your feathers be not drawn for hastiness, but pared even and straight with diligence. The fletcher draweth a feather when it hath but one swap at it with his knife, and then plaineth it a little, with rubbing it over his knife. He pareth it when he taketh leisure and heed to make every part of the rib apt to stand straight and even on upon the stele. This thing if a man take not heed on, he may chance have cause to say so of his fletcher, as in dressing of meat is commonly said of cooks; and that is, that God sendeth ns good feathers, but the devil naughty fletchers. If any fletchers heard me say thus, they would not be angry with me, except they were ill fletchers; and yet by reason, those fletchers too ought rather to amend themselves for doing ill, than be angry with me for saying truth. The rib in a stiff feather may be thinner, for so it will stand cleaner on; but in a weak feather you must leave a thicker rib, or else if the rib, which is the foundation and ground wherein nature hath set every cleft of the feather, be taken too near the feather, it must needs follow, that the feather shall fall and droop down, even as any herb doth which hath his root too near taken on with a spade. The length and shortness of the feather serveth for divers shafts, as a long feather for a long, heavy, or big shaft, the short feather for the contrary. Again, the short may stand farther, the long nearer the nock. Your feather must stand almost straight on, but yet after that sort, that it may turn round in flying.

And here I consider the wonderful nature of shooting, which standeth altogether by that fashion which is most apt for quick moving, and that is by roundness. For first the bow must be gathered round, in drawing it must come round compass, the string must be round, the stele must be round, the best nock round, the feather shorn somewhat round, the shaft in flying must turn round; and, if it fly far, it flieth a round compass, for either above or beneath a round compass hindereth the flying. Moreover, both the fletcher in making your shaft, and you in nocking your shaft, must take heed that two feathers equally run on the bow. For if one feather run alone on the bow, it shall quickly be worn, and shall not be able to match with the other feathers; and again, at the loose, if the shaft be light, it will start; if it be heavy, it will hobble. And thus as concerning setting on of your feather. Now of couling.

To sheer a shaft high or low, must be as the shaft is, heavy or light, great or little, long or short; the swine-backed fashion maketh the shaft deader, for it gathereth more air than the saddle-backed; and therefore the saddle-back is surer for danger of weather, and fitter for smooth flying. Again, to sheer a shaft round, as they were wont sometimes to do, or after the triangle fashion, which is much used now-a-days, both be good. For roundness is apt for flying of his own nature, and all manner of triangle fashion, (the sharp point going before) is also naturally apt for quick entering; and therefore saith Cicero, that cranes, taught by nature, observe in flying a triangle fashion always, because it is so apt to pierce and go through the air withal. Last of all, plucking of feathers is nought, for there is no surety in it; therefore let every archer have such shafts, that he may both know them and trust them at every change of weather. Yet, if they must needs be plucked, pluck them as little as can be, for so shall they be the less unconstant. And thus I have knit up in as short a room as I could, the best feathers, feathering, and couling of a shaft.

Phi. I think surely you have so taken up the matter with you, that you have left nothing behind you. Now you have brought a shaft to the head, which, if it were on, we had done as concerning all instruments belonging to shooting.

Tox. Necessity, the inventor of all goodness (as all authors in a manner do say), amongst all other things made it of strong matter, to last better: last of all, invented a shaft head, first to save the end from breaking; then it made it sharp, to stick better; after it made it of strong matter to last better: last of all, experience and wisdom of men hath brought it to such a perfectness, that there is no one thing so profitable belonging to artillery, either to strike a man's enemy sorer in war, or to shoot nearer the mark at home, than is a fit head for both purposes. For if a shaft lack a head, it is worth nothing for neither use. Therefore, seeing heads be so necessary, they must of necessity be well looked upon. Heads for war, of long time hath been made, not only of divers matters, but also of divers fashions. The Trojans had heads of iron, as this verse, spoken of Pandarus, showeth;

Up to the pap his string did he pull, his shaft to the hard iron.

The Grecians had heads of brass, as Ulysses' shafts were headed, when he slew Antoninus and the other wooers of Penelope.

—Quite through a door flew a shaft with a brass head.

It is plain in Homer, where Menelaus was wounded of Pandarus shafts, that the heads were not glued on, but tied on with a string, as the commentaries in Greek plainly tell. And therefore shooters, at that time, used to carry their shafts without heads, until they occupied them, and then set on an head; as it appear-eth in Homer, the twenty-first book Odyssei, where Penelope brought Ulixes bow down amongst the gentlemen which came on wooing to her, that he which was able to bend it and draw it might enjoy her; and after her followed a maid, saith Homer, carrying a bag full of heads, both of iron and brass.

The men of Scythia used heads of brass. The men of Inde used heads of iron. The Ethiopians used heads of a hard sharp stone, as both Herodotus and Pollux do tell. The Germans, as Cornelius Tacitus doth say, had their shafts headed with bone; and many countries, both of old time and now, use heads of horn. But, of all other, iron and steel must needs be the fittest for heads. Julius Pollux calleth otherwise than we do, where the feathers be the head, and that which we call the head, he calleth the point.

Fashion of heads is divers, and that of old time: two manner of arrow heads, saith Pollux, was used in old time. The one he calleth ὄγκινος, describing it thus, having two points or barbs, looking backward to the stele and the feathers, which surely we call in English a broad arrow head, or a swallow tail. The other he calleth γλῶχις, having two points stretching forward, and this Englishmen do call a fork head; both these two kinds of heads were used in Homer's days; for Teucer used forked heads, saying thus to Agamemnon:
Eight good shafts have I shot sith I came, each one with a fork head.

Pandarus heads and Ulysses' heads were broad arrow heads, as a man may learn in Homer, that would be curious in knowing that matter. Hercules used forked heads, but yet they had three points or forks, when other men's had but two. The Parthians at that great battle where they slew rich Crassus and his son, used broad arrow heads, which stuck so sore that the Romans could not pull them out again. Commodus the Emperor used forked heads, whose fashion Herodian doth lively and naturally describe, saying, that they were like the shape of a new moon, wherewith he would smite off the head of a bird, and never miss: other fashion of heads have not I read on. Our English heads be better in war than either forked heads or broad arrow heads. For first, the end being lighter, they fly a great deal the faster, and, by the same reason, giveth a far sorer stripe. Yea, and I suppose, if the same little barbs which they have were clean put away, they should be far better. For this every man doth grant, that a shaft, as long as it flieth, turns, * and when it leaveth turning, it leaveth going any further. And everything that enters by a turning and boring fashion, the more flatter it is, the worse it enters; as a knife, though it be sharp, yet, because of the edges, will not bore so well as a bodkin, for every round thing enters best; and therefore nature, saith Aristotle, made the rain-drops round, for quick piercing the air. Thus, either shafts turn not in flying, or else our flat arrow heads stop the shaft in entering.

Phi. But yet, Toxophile, to hold your communication a little, I suppose the flat head is better, both because it maketh a greater hole, and also because it sticks faster in.

Tox. These two reasons, as they be both true, so they be both naught. For first, the less hole, if it be deep, is the worse to heal again: when a man shooteth at his enemy, he desireth rather that it should enter far, than stick fast. For what remedy is it, I pray you, for him which is smitten with a deep wound, to pull out the shaft quickly, except it be to haste his death speedily? Thus heads which make a little hole and deep, be better in war, than those which make a great hole and stick fast in. Julius Pollux maketh mention of certain kinds of heads for war, which bear fire in them, and Scripture also speaketh somewhat of the same. Herodotus doth tell a wonderful policy to be done by Xerxes, what time he besieged the great tower in Athens: he made his archers bind their shaft heads about with tow, and then set it on fire and shoot them; which thing done by many archers, set all the places on fire, which were of matter to burn; and, besides that, dazed the men within, so that they knew not whither to turn them. But, to make an end of all heads for war, I would wish that the head-makers of England should make their sheaf-arrow heads more harder pointed than they be: for I myself have seen of late such heads set upon sheaf-arrows, as the officers, if they had seen them, would not have been content withal.

Now as concerning heads for pricking, which is our purpose, there be divers kinds; some be blunt heads, some sharp, some both blunt and sharp. The blunt heads men use, because they perceive them to be good to keep a length withal; they keep a good length, because a man pulleth them no further at one time than at another; for in feeling the plump end always equally, he may loose them. Yet, in a wind, and against the wind, the weather hath so much power on the broad end, that no man can keep no sure length with such a head; therefore a blunt head, in a calm or down a wind, is very good, otherwise none worse. Sharp heads at the end, without any shoulders, (I call that the shoulder in a head which a man's finger shall feel afore it comes to the point,) will perch quickly through a wind; but yet it hath two discommodities; the one that it will keep no length; it keepeth no length, because no man can pull it certainly as far one time as at another: it is not drawn certainly so far one time as at another, because it lacketh shouldering, wherewith, as with a sure token, a man might be warned when to loose; and also because men are afraid of the sharp point for setting it in the bow. The second incommodity is, when it is lighted on the ground, the small point shall at every time be in jeopardy of hurting, which thing, of all other, will soonest make the shaft lose the length. Now, when blunt heads be good to keep a length withal, yet naught for a wind; sharp heads good to perch the weather withal, yet naught for a length; certain head-makers dwelling in London, perceiving the commodity of both kind of heads joined with a discommodity, invented new files and other instruments, wherewith they brought heads for pricking to such a perfectness, that all the commodities of the two other heads should be put in one head, without any discommodity at all. They made a certain kind of heads, which men call high-rigged, creased, or shouldered heads, or silver-spoon heads, for a certain likeness that such heads have with the

knob end of some silver spoons. These heads be good both
to keep a length withal, and also to perch a wind withal. To
keep a length withal, because a man may certainly pull it to
the shouldering every shoot, and no further; to perch a wind
withal, because the point, from the shoulder forward, breaketh
the weather, as all other sharp things do. So the blunt shoulder
serveth for a sure length keeping, the point also is ever fit for a
rough and great weather piercing. And thus much, as shortly
as I could, as concerning heads both for war and peace.

Phi. But is there no cunning as concerning setting on of
the head?

Tox. Well remembered. But that point belongeth to
fletchers; yet you may desire him to set your head full on, and
close on. Full on, is when the wood is bet [*beat*] hard up to
the end or stopping of the head; close on, is when there is left
wood on every side the shaft enough to fill the head withal, or
when it is neither too little nor yet too great. If there be any
fault in any of these points, the head, when it lighteth on any
hard stone, or ground, will be in jeopardy, either of breaking,
or else otherwise hurting. Stopping of heads, either with lead
or any thing else, shall not need now, because every silver
spoon, or shouldered head, is stopped of itself. Short heads be
better than long: for first, the long head is worse for the maker
to file straight compass every way; again, it is worse for the
fletcher to set straight on; thirdly, it is always in more jeopardy
of breaking when it is on. And now, I trow, Philologe, we have

done as concerning all instruments belonging to shooting, which every sere archer ought to provide for himself. And there remaineth two things behind, which be general or common to every man, the weather and the mark; but, because they be so knit with shooting straight, or keeping of a length, I will defer them to that place; and now we will come (God willing) to handle our instruments, the thing that every man desireth to do well.

Phi. If you teach me so well to handle these instruments as you have described them, I suppose I shall be an archer good enough.

Tox. To learn any thing, (as you know better than I, Philologe,) and specially to do a thing with a man's hands, must be done, if a man would be excellent, in his youth. Young trees in gardens, which lack all senses, and beasts without reason, when they be young, may, with handling and teaching, be brought to wonderful things.

And this is not only true in natural things, but in artificial things too; as the potter most cunningly doth cast his pots when his clay is soft and workable, and wax taketh print when it is warm, and leathie weak, not when clay and wax be hard and old: and even so, every man in his youth, both with wit and body, is most apt and pliable to receive any cunning that should be taught him.

This communication of teaching youth, maketh me

remember the right worshipful, and my singular good master, Sir Humphrey Wingfield, to whom, next God, I ought to refer, for his manifold benefits bestowed on me, the poor talent of learning which God hath lent me; and for his sake do I owe my service to all other of the name and noble house of the Wingfields, both in word and deed. This worshipful man hath ever loved and used to have many children brought up in learning in his house, amongst whom I myself was one. For whom at term-times he would bring down from London both bow and shafts; and, when they should play, he would go with them himself into the field, and see them shoot; and he that shot fairest, should have the best bow and shafts; and he that shot ill-favouredly should be mocked of his fellows, till he shot better.

Would to God all England had used, or would use, to lay the foundation, after the example of this worshipful man, in bringing up children in the book and the bow! by which two things the whole commonwealth, both in peace and war, is chiefly ruled and defended withal.

But to our purpose: He that must come to this high perfectness in shooting, which we speak of, must needs begin to learn it in his youth; the omitting of which thing in England, both maketh fewer shooters, and also every man, that is a shooter, shoot worse than he might if he were taught.

Phi. Even as I know that this is true which you say, even so, Toxophile, have you quite discouraged me, and drawn my mind clean from shooting; seeing, by this reason, no man that hath not used it in his youth can be excellent in it. And I suppose the same reason would discourage many other mo, if they heard you talk after this sort.

Tox. This thing, Philologe, shall discourage no man that is wise. For I will prove that wisdom may work the same thing in a man, that nature doth in a child.

A child by three things is brought to excellency. By aptness, desire, and fear: aptness maketh him pliable, like wax, to be formed and fashioned, even as a man would have him. Desire, to be as good, or better than his fellows; and fear of them whom he is under, will cause him take great labour and pain with diligent heed in learning any thing, whereof proceedeth, at the last, excellency and perfectness.

A man may, by wisdom in learning any thing, and specially to shoot, have three like commodities also, whereby he may, as it were, become young again, and so attain to excellency. For as a child is apt by natural youth, so a man by using at the first weak bows, far underneath his strength, shall be as pliable and ready to be taught fair shooting as any child; and daily use of the same shall both keep him in fair shooting, and also at the last bring him to strong shooting.

And, instead of the fervent desire which provoketh a child to be better than his fellow, let a man be as much stirred up with shamefacedness to be worse than all other. And the same place that fear hath in a child, to compel him to take pain, the same hath love of shooting in a man, to cause him forsake no labour, without which no man nor child can be excellent. And thus, whatsoever a child may be taught by aptness, desire, and fear, the same thing in shooting may a man be taught by weak bows, shamefacedness, and love.

And hereby you may see that that is true which Cicero saith; that a man, by use, may be brought to a new nature. And this I dare be bold to say, that any man which will wisely begin, and constantly persevere in this trade of learning to shoot, shall attain to perfectness therein.

Phi. This communication, Toxophile, doth please me very well; and now I perceive that most generally and chiefly youth must be taught to shoot; and, secondarily, no man is debarred therefrom, except it be more through his own negligence, for because he will not learn, than any disability because he cannot learn. Therefore, seeing I will be glad to follow your counsel in choosing my bow and other instruments, and also am ashamed that I can shoot no better than I can; moreover, having such a love toward shooting by your good reasons to-day, that I will forsake no labour in the exercise of the same; I beseech you imagine that we had both bow and shafts here, and teach me how I should handle them; and one thing I desire you, make me as fair an archer as you can.

For this I am sure, in learning all other matters, nothing is brought to the most profitable use, which is not handled after the most comely fashion. As masters of fence have no stroke fit either to hit another, or else to defend himself, which is not joined with a wonderful comeliness. A cook cannot chop his herbs neither quickly nor handsomely, except he keep such a measure with his chopping-knives, as would delight a man both to see him and hear him. Every handcraftman that works best for his own profit, works most seemly to other men's sight. Again, in building a house, in making a ship, every part, the more handsomely they be joined for profit and last,* the more comely they be fashioned to every man's sight and eye.

Nature itself taught men to join always well-favouredness with profitableness. As in man, that joint or piece which is by any chance deprived of his comeliness, the same is also debarred of his use and profitableness. And he that is goggle-eyed, and looks asquint, hath both his countenance clean marred, and his sight sore blemished; and so in all other members like. Moreover what time of the year bringeth most profit with it for man's use, the same also covereth and decketh both earth and trees with most comeliness for man's pleasure. And that time which taketh away the pleasure of the ground, carrieth with him also the profit of the ground, as every man by experience knoweth in hard and rough winters. Some things there be which have no other end but only comeliness, as painting and dancing. And virtue itself is nothing else but comeliness, as all philosophers do agree in opinion; therefore seeing that which is best done in any matters, is always most comely done, as both Plato and Cicero in many places do prove, and daily experience doth teach in other things, I pray you, as I said before, teach me to shoot as fair, well-favouredly, as you can imagine.

Tox. Truly, Philologe, as you prove very well in other matters, the best shooting is always the most comely shooting; but this you know, as well as I, that Crassus showeth in Cicero, that, as comeliness is the chief point, and most to be sought for in all things, so comeliness only can never be taught by any art or craft; but may be perceived well when it is done, not described well how it should be done. Yet, nevertheless, to come to it there be many ways, which wise men have assayed in other matters; as if a man would follow, in learning to shoot fair, the noble painter Zeuxes in painting Helena, which, to make his image beautiful, did choose out five of the fairest maids in all the country about; and in beholding them, conceived and drew out such an image, that it far exceeded all other, because the comeliness of them all was brought into one most perfect comeliness: so likewise in shooting, if a man would set before his eyes five or six of the fairest archers that ever he saw shoot, and of one learn to stand, of another to draw, of another to loose, and so take of every man what every man could do best; I dare say, he should come to such a comeliness as never man came to yet. As for an example, if the most comely point in shooting that Hewe Prophete the king's servant hath, and as my friends Thomas and Ralph Cantrell doth use with the most seemly fashions that three or four excellent archers have beside, were all joined in one, I am sure all men would wonder at the excellency of it. And this is one way to learn to shoot fair.

Phi. This is very well, truly; but I pray you teach me somewhat of shooting fair yourself.

Tox. I can teach you to shoot fair, even as Socrates taught a man once to know God: for, when he axed [*asked*] him what was God, nay, saith he, I can tell you better what God is not; as, God is not ill, God is unspeakable, unsearchable, and so forth: even likewise can I say of fair shooting, it hath not this discommodity with it nor that discommodity; and, at last, a man may so shift all the discommodities from shooting, that there shall be left nothing behind but fair shooting. And to do this the better, you must remember how that I told you, when I described generally the whole nature of shooting, that fair shooting came of these things, of standing, nocking, drawing, holding, and loosing; the which I will go over as shortly as I can, describing the discommodities that men commonly use in all parts of their bodies; that you, if you fault in any such, may know it, and so go about to amend it. Faults in archers do exceed the number of archers, which come with use of shooting without teaching. Use and custom separated from knowledge and learning, doth not only hurt shooting, but the most weighty things in the world beside; and, therefore, I marvel much at those people which be the maintainers of uses without knowledge, having no other word in their mouth but this, Use, use, Custom, custom. Such men, more wilful than wise, beside other discommodities, take all place and occasion from all amendment. And this I speak generally of use and custom. Which thing, if a learned man had it in hand that would apply it to any one matter, he might handle it wonderfully. But, as for shooting, use is the only cause of all faults in it; and therefore children more easily and sooner may be taught to shoot excellently than men, because children may be taught to shoot well at the first, men have more pain to unlearn their ill uses, than they have labour afterward to come to good shooting.

All the discommodities which ill custom hath graffed in archers, can neither be quickly pulled out, nor yet soon reckoned of me, they be so many. Some shooteth his head forward, as though he would bite the mark; another stareth with his eyes, as though they should fly out; another winketh with one eye and looketh with the other; some make a face with writhing their mouth and countenance so, as though they were doing you wot what; another bleareth out his tongue; another biteth his lips; another holdeth his neck awry. In drawing some fet such a compass, as though they would turn about, and bless* all the field; other heave their hand now up now down, that a man cannot discern whereat they would shoot: another waggeth the upper end of his bow one way, the nether end another way. Another will stand pointing his shaft at the mark a good while, and, by and by, he will give him a whip, and away or a man wit. Another maketh such a wrestling with his gear, as though he were able to shoot no more as long as he lived. Another draweth softly to the midst, and, by and by, it is gone you cannot know how. Another draweth his shaft low at the breast, as though he would shoot at a roving mark, and by and by, he lifteth his arm up prick height. Another maketh a wrenching with his back, as though a man pinched him behind. Another cowereth down, and lay-eth out his buttocks, as though he should shoot at crows. Another setteth forward his left leg, and draweth back with head and shoulders, as though he pulled at a rope, or else were afraid of the mark. Another draweth his shaft well, until within two fingers of the head, and then he stayeth a little, to look at his mark, and, that done, pulleth it up to the head, and looseth; which way, although some excellent shooters do use, yet surely it is a fault, and good men's faults are not to be followed. Some men draw too far, some too short, some too slowly, some too quickly; some hold over-long, some let go over-soon. Some set their shaft on the ground, and fetcheth him upward; another pointeth up toward the sky, and so bringeth him downwards.

Once I saw a man which used a bracer on his cheek, or else he had scratched all the skin of the one side of his face with his drawing-hand. Another I saw which, at every shot, after the loose, lifted up his right leg so far that he was ever in jeopardy of falling. Some stamp forward, and some leap backward. All these faults be either in the drawing, or at the loose; with many other mo, which you may easily perceive, and so go about to avoid them.

Now afterward, when the shaft is gone, men have many faults, which evil custom hath brought them to; and specially in crying after the shaft, and speaking words scarce honest for such an honest pastime.

Such words be very tokens of an ill mind, and manifest signs of a man that is subject to immeasurable affections. Good men's ears do abhor them, and an honest man therefore will avoid them. And besides those which must needs have their tongue thus walking, other men use other faults, as some will take their bow and writhe and wrench it, to pull in his shaft, when it flieth wide, as if he drave a cart. Some will give two or three strides forward, dancing and hopping after his shaft, as long as it flieth, as though he were a mad man. Some, which fear to be too far gone, run backward, as it were to pull his shaft back. Another runneth forward, when he feareth to be short, heaving after his arms, as though he would help his shaft to fly. Another writhes or runneth aside, to pull in his shaft straight. One lifteth up his heel, and so holdeth his foot still, as long as his shaft flieth. Another casteth his arm backward after the loose. And another swings his bow about him, as it were a man with a shaft to make room in a game place. And many other faults there be, which now come not to my remembrance. Thus, as you have heard, many archers, with marring their face and countenance, with other parts of their body, as it were men that should dance anticks, be far from the comely port in shooting, which he that would be excellent must look for.

Of these faults I have very many myself; but I talk not of my shooting, but of the general nature of shooting. Now imagine an archer that is clean without all these faults, and I am sure every man would be delighted to see him shoot.

And although such a perfect comeliness cannot be expressed with any precept of teaching, as Cicero and other learned men do say, yet I will speak (according to my little knowledge) that thing in it, which if you follow, although you shall not be without fault, yet your fault shall neither quickly be perceived, nor yet greatly rebuked of them that stand by. Standing, nocking, drawing, holding, loosing, done as they should be done, make fair shooting.

The first point is, when a man should shoot to take such footing and standing, as shall be both comely to the eye and profitable to his use, setting his countenance and all the other parts of his body after such a behaviour and port, that both all his strength may be employed to his own most advantage, and his shoot made and handled to other men's pleasure and delight. A man must not go too hastily to it, for that is rashness, nor yet make too much to do about it, for that is curiosity; the one foot must not stand too far from the other, lest he stoop too much, which is unseemly, nor yet too near together, lest he stand too straight up, for so a man shall neither use his strength well, nor yet stand stedfastly.

The mean betwixt both must be kept; a thing more pleasant to behold when it is done, than easy to be taught how it should be done.

To nock well is the easiest point of all, and therein is no cunning, but only diligent heed-giving, to set his shaft neither too high nor too low, but even straight overthwart his bow. Unconstant nocking maketh a man loose his length. And besides that, if the shaft hand be high, and the bow hand low, or contrary, both the bow is in jeopardy of breaking, and the shaft, if it be little, will start; if it be great, it will hobble. Knock the cock feather upward always, as I told you when I described the feather. And be sure always that your string slip not out of the nock, for then all is in jeopardy of breaking.

Drawing well is the best part of shooting. Men in old time used other manner of drawing than we do. They used to draw low at the breast, to the right pap, and no further; and this to be true is plain in Homer, when he describeth Pandarus shooting:

Up to the pap his string did he pull, his shaft to the hard head.

The noble women of Scythia used the same fashion of

shooting low at the breast, and, because their left pap hindered their shooting at the loose, they cut it off when they were young, and therefore they be called, in lacking their pap, Amazones. Now-a-day, contrariwise, we draw to the right ear, and not to the pap. Whether the old way in drawing low to the pap, or the new way to draw aloft to the ear, be better, an excellent writer in Greek, called Procopius, doth say his mind, showing that the old fashion in drawing to the pap was nought, of no pith, and therefore, saith Procopius, is artillery dispraised in Homer, which calleth it **οὐτίδανον**, i. e. weak, and able to do no good. Drawing to the ear he praiseth greatly, whereby men shoot both stronger and longer: drawing therefore to the ear is better than to draw at the breast. And one thing cometh into my remembrance now, Philologe, when I speak of drawing, that I never read of other kind of shooting, than drawing with a man's hand either to the breast or ear: this thing have I sought for in Homer, Herodotus, and Plutarch, and therefore I marvel how crossbows came first up, of the which, I am sure, a man shall find little mention made in any good author. Leo the Emperor would have his soldiers draw quickly in war, for that maketh a shaft fly apace. In shooting at the pricks, hasty and quick drawing is neither sure nor yet comely. Therefore to draw easily and uniformly, that is for to say, not wagging your hand, now upward, now downward, but always after one fashion, until you come to the rig or shouldering of the head, is best both for profit and seemliness. Holding must not be long, for it both putteth a bow in jeopardy, and also marreth a man's shoot; it must be so little, that it may be perceived better in a man's mind when it is done, than seen with a man's eyes when it is in doing. Loosing must be much like. So quick and hard, that it be without all girds; so soft and gentle, that the shaft fly not as it were sent out of a bow-case. The mean betwixt both, which is perfect loosing, is not so hard to be followed in shooting as it is to be described in teaching. For clean loosing, you must take heed of hitting any thing about you. And for the same purpose, Leo the Emperor would have all archers in war to have both their heads polled, and their beards shaven, lest the hair of their heads should stop the sight of the eye, the hair of their beards hinder the course of the string. And these precepts I am sure, Philologe, if you follow, in standing, nocking, drawing, holding, and loosing, shall bring you at the last to excellent fair shooting.

Phi. All these things, Toxophile, although I both now perceive them thoroughly, and also will remember them diligently; yet to-morrow, or some other day when you have leisure, we will go to the pricks, and put them by little and little in experience. For teaching not followed, doeth even as much good as books never looked upon. But now, seeing you have taught me to shoot fair, I pray you tell me somewhat, how I should shoot near, lest that proverb might be said justly of me some time, "He shoots like a gentleman fair and far off."

Tox. He that can shoot fair, lacketh nothing but shooting straight, and keeping of a length, whereof cometh hitting of the mark, the end both of shooting, and also of this our communication. The handling of the weather and the mark, because they belong to shooting straight and keeping of a length, I will join them together, showing what things belong to keeping of a length, and what to shooting straight.

The greatest enemy of shooting is the wind and the weather, whereby true keeping a length is chiefly hindered. If this thing were not, men, by teaching, might be brought to wonderful near shooting. It is no marvel if the little poor shaft, being sent alone so high into the air, into a great rage of weather, one wind tossing it that way, another this way; it is no marvel, I say, though it leese [*lose*] the length, and miss that place where the shooter had thought to have found it. Greater matters than shooting are under the rule and will of the weather, as sailing on the sea. And likewise, as in sailing, the chief point of a good master is to know the tokens of change of weather, the course of the winds, that thereby he may the better come to the haven: even so the best property of a good shooter is to know the nature of the winds, with him and against him, and thereby he may the nearer shoot at his mark. Wise masters, when they cannot win the best haven, they are glad of the next: good shooters also, that cannot when they would hit the mark, will labour to come as nigh as they can. All things in this world be unperfect and unconstant;

therefore let every man acknowledge his own weakness in all matters, great and small, weighty and merry, and glorify Him in whom only perfect perfectness is. But now, Sir, he that will at all adventures use the seas, knowing no more what is to be done in a tempest than in a calm, shall soon become a merchant of eel-skins: so that shooter which putteth no difference, but shooteth in all alike, in rough weather and fair, shall always put his winnings in his eyes, Little boats and thin boards cannot endure the rage of a tempest. Weak bows and light shafts cannot stand in a rough wind. And likewise as a blind man, which should go to a place where he had never been before, that hath but one straight way to it, and of either side holes and pits to fall into, now falleth into this hole, and then into that hole, and never cometh to his journey's end, but wandereth always here and there, farther and farther off; so that archer which ignorantly shooteth, considering neither fair nor foul, standing nor nocking, feather nor head, drawing nor loosing, nor any compass, shall always shoot short and gone, wide and far off, and never come near, except perchance he stumble sometime on the mark. For ignorance is nothing else but mere blindness.

A master of a ship first learneth to know the coming of a tempest, the nature of it, and how to behave himself in it, either with changing his course, or pulling down his high tops and broad sails, being glad to eschew as much of the weather as he can; even so a good archer will first, with diligent use and marking the weather learn to know the nature of the wind; and, with wisdom, will measure in his mind, how much it will alter his shot, either in length, keeping, or else in straight shooting; and so, with changing his standing, or taking another shaft, the which he knoweth perfectly to be better for his purpose, either because it is lower feathered, or else because it is of a better wing, will so handle with discretion his shot, that he shall seem rather to have the weather under his rule, by good heed-giving, than the weather to rule his shaft by any sudden changing.

Therefore, in shooting, there is as much difference betwixt an archer that is a good weather man, and another that knoweth and marketh nothing, as is betwixt a blind man and he that can see.

Thus, as concerning the weather, a perfect archer must first learn to know the sure flight of his shafts, that he may be bold always to trust them; then must he learn by daily experience all manner of kinds of weather, the tokens of it, when it will come, the nature of it when it is come; the diversity and altering of it when it changeth, the decrease and diminishing of it when it ceaseth. Thirdly, these things known and every shot diligently marked, then must a man compare always the weather and his footing together, and with discretion, measure them so that whatsoever the weather shall take away from his shoot, the same shall just footing restore again to his shoot. This thing well known, and discreetly handled in shooting, bringeth more profit and commendation and praise to an archer, than any other thing besides. He that would know perfectly the wind and weather, must put differences betwixt times. For diversity of time causeth diversity of weather, as in the whole year; spring time, summer, fall of the leaf, and winter: likewise in one day, morning, noontide, afternoon, and eventide, both alter the weather, and change a man's bow with the strength of man also. And to know that this is so, is enough for a shooter and artillery, and not to search the cause why it should be so: which belongeth to a learned man and philosophy. In considering the time of the year, a wise archer will follow a good shipman; in winter and rough weather, small boats and little pinks forsake the seas: and at one time of the year no galleys come abroad: so likewise weak archers using small and hollow shafts, with bows of little pith must be content to give place for a time. And this I do not say, either to discourage any weak shooter; for likewise, as there is no ship better than galleys be in a soft and a calm sea, so no man shooteth comelier, or nearer his mark, than some weak archers do in a fair and clear day.

Thus every archer must know, not only what bow and shaft is fittest for him to shoot withal, but also what time and season is best for him to shoot in. And surely, in all other matters too, among all degrees of men, there is no man which doth any thing either more discreetly for his commendation, or yet more profitable for his advantage than he which will know perfectly for what matter, and for what time he is most apt and fit. If men would go about matters which they should do, and be fit for, not such things which wilfully they desire, and yet be unfit for, verily greater matters in the commonwealth than shooting should be in better case than they be. This ignorancy in men which know not for what time, and to what thing they be fit, causeth some wish to be rich, for whom it were better a great deal to be poor; other to be meddling in every man's matter, for whom it were more honesty to be quiet and still. Some to desire to be in the court, which be born and be fitter rather for the cart. Some to be masters and rule other, which never yet began to rule themselves; some always to jangle and talk, which rather should hear and keep silence. Some to teach which rather should learn. Some to be priests which were fitter to be clerks. And this perverse judgment of the world, when men measure themselves amiss, bringeth much disorder and great unseemliness to the whole body of the commonwealth; as if a man should wear his hose upon his head, or a woman go with a sword and a buckler, every man would take it as a great uncomeliness, although it be but a trifle in respect of the other.

This perverse judgment of men hindereth nothing so much as learning, because commonly those which be un-fittest for learning, be chiefly set to learning. As if a man now-a-days have two sons, the one impotent, weak, sickly, lisping, stuttering, and stammering, or having any mis-shape in his body; what doth the father of such one commonly say? This boy is fit for nothing else but to set to learning and make a priest of; as who would say the outcasts of the world, having neither countenance, tongue, nor wit, (for of a perverse body cometh commonly a perverse mind,) be good enough to make those men of, which shall be appointed to preach God's holy word, and minister his blessed sacraments, besides other most weighty matters in the commonwealth, put oftimes, and worthily, to learned men's discretion and charge; when rather such an office, so high in dignity, so godly in administration, should be committed to no man, which should not have a countenance full of comeliness to allure good men, a body full of manly authority to fear* ill men, a wit apt for all learning, with tongue and voice able to persuade all men. And although few such men as these can be found in a commonwealth, yet surely a godly disposed man will both in his mind think fit, and with all his study labour to get such men as I speak of, or rather better, if better can be gotten, for such an high administration, which is most properly appointed to God's own matters and businesses.

This perverse judgment of fathers, as concerning the fitness and unfitness of their children, causeth the commonwealth have many unfit ministers; and seeing that ministers be, as a man would say, instruments wherewith the commonwealth doth work all her matters withal, I marvel how it chanceth that a poor shoemaker hath so much wit, that he will prepare no instrument for his science, neither knife nor awl, nor nothing else, which is not very fit for him: the commonwealth can be content to take at a fond father's hand the rif raff of the world to make those instruments of, wherewithal she should work the highest matters under heaven. And surely an awl of lead is not so unprofitable in a shoemaker's shop, as an unfit minister, made of gross metal, is unseemly in the commonwealth. Fathers in old time among the noble Persians might not do with their children as they thought good, but as the judgment of the commonwealth always thought best. This fault of fathers bringeth many a blot with it, to the great deformity of the commonwealth; and here surely I can praise gentlewomen, which have always at hand their glasses, to see if any thing be amiss, and so will amend it; yet the commonwealth, having the glass of knowledge in every man's hand, doth see such uncomeliness in it and yet winketh at it. This fault, and many such like, might be soon wiped away, if fathers would bestow their children on that thing always, whereunto nature hath ordained them most apt and fit. For if youth be grafted straight, and not awry, the whole commonwealth will flourish thereafter. When this is done, then must every man begin to be more ready to amend himself than to check another, measuring their matters with that wise proverb of Apollo, "Know thyself:" that is to say, learn to know what thou art able, fit and apt unto, and follow that. This thing should be both comely to the commonwealth, and most profitable for every one; as doth appear very well in all wise men's deeds, and specially (to turn to our communication again) in shooting, where wise archers have always their instruments fit for their strength, and wait evermore such time and weather as is most agreeable to their gear. Therefore, if the weather be too sore, and unfit for your shooting, leave off for that day, and wait a better season. For he is a fool that will not go whom necessity driveth.

Phi. This communication of yours pleased me so well, Toxophile, that surely I was not hasty to call you to describe forth the weather, but with all my heart would have suffered you yet to have stood longer in this matter. For these things touched of you by chance, and by the way, be far above the matter itself, by whose occasion the other were brought in.

Tox. Weighty matters they be indeed, and fit both in another place to be spoken, and of another man than I am to be handled. And, because mean men must meddle with mean matters, I will go forward in describing the weather as concerning shooting: and, as I told you before, in the whole year, spring-time, summer, fall of the leaf, and winter; and in one day, morning, noon-time, afternoon, and eventide, altereth the course of the weather, the pith of the bow, the strength of the man. And in every one of these times, the weather altereth; as sometime windy, sometime calm, sometime cloudy, sometime clear, sometime hot, sometime cold, the wind sometime moisty and thick, sometime dry and smooth. A little wind in a moisty day stoppeth a shaft more than a good whisking wind in a clear day. Yea, and I have seen when there hath been no wind at all, the air so misty and thick, that both the marks have been wonderful great. And once, when the plague was in Cambridge, the down wind* twelve score mark for the space of three weeks was thirteen score and an half, and into the wind, being not very great, a great deal above fourteen score.

The wind is sometime plain up and down, which is commonly most certain, and requireth least knowledge, wherein a mean shooter, with mean gear, if he can shoot home, may make best shift. A side wind trieth an archer and good gear very much. Sometime it bloweth aloft, sometime hard by the ground; sometime it bloweth by blasts, and sometime it continueth all in one; sometime full side wind, sometime quarter with him, and more; and likewise against him, as a man with casting up light grass, or else if he take good heed, shall sensibly learn by experience. To see the wind with a man his eyes it is unpossible, the nature of it is so fine and subtile; yet this experience of the wind had I once myself, and that was in the great snow that fell four years ago. I rode in the high way betwixt Topcliff-upon-Swale and Boroughbridge, the way being somewhat trodden before, by way-faring men; the fields on both sides were plain, and lay almost yard-deep with snow; the night afore had been a little frost, so that the snow was hard and crusted above; that morning the sun shone bright and clear, the wind was whistling aloft, and sharp, according to the time of the year; the snow in the high way lay loose and trodden with horses' feet; so as the wind blew, it took the loose snow with it, and made it so slide upon the snow in the field, which was hard and crusted by reason of the frost over night, that thereby I might see very well the whole nature of the wind as it blew that day. And I had a great delight and pleasure to mark it, which maketh me now far better to remember it. Sometime the wind would be not past two yards broad, and so it would carry the snow as far as I could see. Another time the snow would blow over half the field at once. Sometime the snow would tumble softly; by and by it would fly wonderful fast. And this I perceived also, that the wind goeth by streams, and not whole together. For I should see one stream within a score on me; then the space of two score, no snow would stir; but, after so much quantity of ground, another stream of snow, at the same very time, should be carried likewise, but not equally, for the one would stand still, when the other flew apace and so continue sometime swiftlier, sometime slowlier, sometime broader, sometime narrower, as far as I could see. Nor it flew not straight, but sometime it crooked this way, sometime that way, and sometime it ran round about in a compass. And sometime the snow would be lift clean from the ground up to the air, and by and by it would be all clapt to the ground, as though there had been no wind at all, straightway it would rise and fly again. And that which was the most marvel of all, at one time two drifts of snow flew, the one out of the west into the east, the other out of the north into the east. And I saw two winds, by reason of the snow, the one cross over the other, as it had been two high ways. And, again, I should hear the wind blow in the air, when nothing was stirred at the ground. And when all was still where I rode, not very far from me the snow should be lifted wonderfully. This experience made me more marvel at the nature of the wind, than it made me cunning in the knowledge of the wind; but yet thereby I learned perfectly that it is no marvel at all though men in wind lose their length in shooting, seeing so many ways the wind is so variable in blowing.

But seeing that a master of a ship, be he never so cunning, by the uncertainty of the wind, loseth many times both life and goods: surely it is no wonder, though a right good archer, by the self same wind, so variable in his own nature, so insensible to our nature, lose many a shoot and game.

The more uncertain and deceivable the wind is, the more heed must a wise archer give to know the guiles of it. He that doth mistrust is seldom beguiled. For although thereby he shall not attain to that which is best, yet by these means he shall at least avoid that which is worst. Beside all these kinds of winds, you must take heed if you see any cloud appear, and gather by little and little against you, or else, if a shower of rain be like to come upon you, for then both the driving of the weather and the thickening of the air increaseth the mark; when, after the shower, all things are contrary clear and calm, and the mark, for the most part, new to begin again. You must take heed also, if ever you shoot where one of the marks, or both, stands a little short of a high wall, for there you may be easily beguiled. If you take grass and cast it up, to see how the wind stands, many times you shall suppose to shoot down the wind, when you shoot clean against the wind. And a good reason why. For the wind which cometh indeed against you, redoundeth back again at the wall, and whirleth back to the prick, and a little farther, and then turneth again, even as a vehement water doth against a rock, or an high bray; which example of water, as it is more sensible to a man's eyes, so it is never a whit the truer than this of the wind. So that the grass cast up shall flee that way which indeed is the longer mark, and deceive quickly a shooter that is not ware of it.

This experience had I once myself at Norwich, in the chapel field within the walls. And this way I used in shooting at those marks. When I was in the mid way betwixt the marks, which was an open place, there I took a feather or a little light grass; and so, as well as I could, learned how the wind stood; that done I went to the prick as fast as I could, and, according as I had found the wind when I was in the mid way, so I was fain then to be content to make the best of my shoot that I could. Even such another experience had I, in a manner, at York, at the pricks lying betwixt the castle and Ouse side. And although you smile, Philologe, to hear me tell mine own fondness; yet, seeing you will needs have me teach you somewhat in shooting, I must needs sometime tell you of mine own experience; and the better I may do so, because Hippocrates, in teaching physic, useth very much the same way. Take heed also when you shoot near the sea coast although you be two or three miles from the sea; for there diligent marking shall espy in the most clear day wonderful changing. The same is to be considered likewise by a river side, especially if it ebb and flow, where he that taketh diligent heed of the tide and weather, shall lightly take away all that he shooteth for. And thus of the nature of winds and weather, according to my marking, you have heard, Philologe: and hereafter you shall mark far mo yourself, if you take heed. And the weather thus marked, as I told you before, you must take heed of your standing, that thereby you may win as much as you shall lose by the weather.

Phi. I see well it is no marvel though a man miss many times in shooting, seeing the weather is so unconstant in blowing; but yet there is one thing which many archers use, that shall cause a man have less need to mark the weather, and that is aim-giving.

Tox. Of giving aim, I cannot tell well what I should say. For in a strange place it taketh away all occasion of foul game, which is the only praise of it; yet by my judgment, it hindereth the knowledge of shooting, and maketh men more negligent;

the which is a dispraise. Though aim be given, yet take heed, for at another man's shot you cannot well take aim, nor at your own neither, because the weather will alter, even in a minute, and at the one mark, and not at the other, and trouble your shaft in the air, when you shall perceive no wind at the ground, as I myself have seen shafts tumble aloft in a very fair day. There may be a fault also in drawing or loosing, and many things mo, which altogether are required to keep a just length. But, to go forward, the next point after the marking of your weather, as the taking of your standing. And, in a side wind, you must stand somewhat cross into the wind, for so shall you shoot the surer. When you have taken good footing, then must you look at your shaft, that no earth, nor wet, be left upon it, for so should it lose the length. You must look at the head also, lest it have had any stripe at the last shoot. A stripe upon a stone, many times will both mar the head, crook the shaft, and hurt the feather, whereof the least of them all will cause a man lose his length. For such things which chance every shoot, many archers use to have some place made in their coat, fit for a little file, a stone, a hunfish skin, and a cloth to dress the shaft fit again at all needs. This must a man look to ever when he taketh up his shaft. And the head may be made too smooth, which will cause it fly too far; when your shaft is fit, then must you take your bow even in the midst, or else you shall both lose your length, and put your bow in jeopardy of breaking. Nocking just is next, which is much of the same nature. Then draw equally, loose equally, with holding your hand ever of one height to keep true compass. To look at your shaft head at the loose is the greatest help to keep a length that can be, which thing yet hindereth excellent shooting, because a man cannot shoot straight perfectly except he look at his mark; if I should shoot at a line, and not at the mark, I would always look at my shaft end; but of this thing somewhat afterward. Now, if you mark the weather diligently, keep your standing justly, hold and nock truly, draw and loose equally, and keep your compass certainly, you shall never miss of your length.

Phi. Then there is nothing behind to make me hit the mark, but only shooting straight.

Tox. No truly. And I first will tell you what shifts archers have found to shoot straight, then what is the best way to shoot straight. As the weather belongeth specially to keep a length (yet a side wind belongeth also to shoot straight) even so the nature of the prick is to shoot straight. The length or shortness of the mark is always under the rule of the weather, yet somewhat there is in the mark, worthy to be marked of an archer. If the pricks stand of a straight plain ground, they be the best to shoot at. If the mark stand on a hill-side or the ground be unequal with pits and turning ways betwixt the marks, a man's eye shall think that to be straight which is crooked; the experience of this thing is seen in painting, the cause of it is known by learning; and it is enough for an archer to mark it, and take heed of it. The chief cause why men cannot shoot straight, is because they look at their shaft; and this fault cometh, because a man is not taught to shoot when he is young. If he learn to shoot by himself, he is afraid to pull the shaft through the bow, and therefore looketh always at his shaft; ill use confirmeth this fault, as it doth many more. And men continue the longer in this fault, because it is so good to keep a length withal: and yet, to shoot straight, they have invented some ways to espy a tree or a hill beyond the mark, or else to have some notable thing betwixt the marks; and once I saw a good archer which did cast off his gear and laid his quiver with it, even in the mid-way betwixt the pricks. Some thought he did it for safeguard of his gear: I suppose he did it to shoot straight withal. Other men use to espy some mark almost a bow wide of the prick, and then go about to keep himself on the hand that the prick is on; which thing how much good it doth, a man will not believe, that doth not prove it. Other, and those very good archers, in drawing, look at the mark until they come almost to the head, then they look at their shaft; but, at the very loose, with a second sight, they find their mark again. This way and all other afore of me rehearsed, are but shifts, and not to be followed in shooting straight. For having a man's eye always on his mark, is the only way to shoot straight; yea, and I suppose, so ready and easy a way, if it be learned in youth, and confirmed with use, that a man shall never miss therein. Men doubt yet in looking at the mark what way is best, whether betwixt the bow and the string, above or beneath his hand, and many ways moo; yet it maketh no great matter which way a man look at his mark, if it be joined with comely shooting. The diversity of men's standing and drawing causeth divers men look at their mark divers ways; yet they all lead a man's hand to shoot straight, if nothing else stop. So that comeliness is the only judge of best looking at the mark. Some men wonder why, in casting a man's eye at the mark, the hand should go straight: surely if he considered the nature of a man's eye, he would not wonder at it: for this I am certain of, that no servant to his master, no child to his father, is so obedient, as every joint and piece of the body is to do whatsoever the eye bids. The eye is the guide, the ruler, and the succourer of all the other parts. The hand, the foot, and other members, dare do nothing without the eye, as doth appear on the night and dark corners. The eye is the very tongue wherewith wit and reason doth speak to every part of the body, and the wit doth not so soon signify a thing by the eye, as every part is ready to follow, or rather prevent the bidding of the eye. This is plain in many things, but most evident in fence and fighting, as I have heard men say. There every part standing in fear to have a blow, runs to the eye for help, as young children do to the mother; the foot, the hand, and all waiteth upon the eye. If the eye bid the hand either bear off or smite, or the foot either go forward or backward, it doth so; and that which is most wonder of all, the one man looking stedfastly at the other man's eye, and not at his hand, will, even as it were, read in his eye where he purposeth to smite next, for the eye is nothing else but a certain window for wit to shoot out her head at.

This wonderful work of God in making all the members so obedient to the eye, is a pleasant thing to remember and look upon; therefore an archer may be sure, in learning to look at his mark when he is young, always to shoot straight. The things that hinder a man which looketh at his mark, to shoot straight, be these: a side wind; a bow either too strong, or else too weak; an ill arm, when a feather runneth on the bow too much; a big-breasted shaft, for him that shooteth under hand, because it will hobble; a little-breasted shaft for him that shooteth above the hand, because it will start; a pair of winding pricks, and many other things moo, which you shall mark yourself, and as ye know them, so learn to amend them. If a man would leave to look at his shaft, and learn to look at his mark, he may use this way, which a good shooter told me once that he did. Let him take his bow on the night, and shoot at two lights, and there he shall be compelled to look always at his mark, and never at his shaft: this thing, once or twice used, will cause him forsake looking at his shaft. Yet let him take heed of setting his shaft in the bow.

Thus, Philologe, to shoot straight is the least mastery of all, if a man order himself thereafter in his youth. And as for keeping a length, I am sure, the rules which I gave you will never deceive you; so that there shall lack nothing, either of hitting the mark always, or else very near shooting, except the fault be only in your own self, which may come two ways, either in having a faint heart or courage, or else in suffering yourself overmuch to be led with affection: if a man's mind fail him, the body, which is ruled by the mind, can never do his duty; if lack of courage were not, men might do mo masteries than they do, as doth appear in leaping and vaulting.

All affections, and specially anger, hurteth both mind and body. The mind is blind thereby, and if the mind be blind, it cannot rule the body aright. The body, both blood and bone, as they say, is brought out of his right course by anger; whereby a man lacketh his right strength, and therefore cannot shoot well. If these things be avoided (whereof I will speak no more, both because they belong not properly to shooting, and also you can teach me better in them than I you), and all the precepts which I have given you diligently marked, no doubt ye shall shoot as well as ever man did yet, by the grace of God.

This communication handled of me, Philologe, as I know well not perfectly, yet, as I suppose, truly, you must take in good worth; wherein if divers things do not altogether please you, thank yourself, which would have me rather fault in mere folly, to take that thing in hand which I was not able for to perform, than by any honest shamefacedness with-say your request and mind, which I know well I have not satisfied.

But yet I will think this labour of mine the better bestowed, if to-morrow, or some other day when you have leisure, you will spend as much time with me here in this same place, in entreating the question *De origine animæ*, and the joining of it with the body, that I may know how far Plato, Aristotle, and the Stoics have waded in it.

Phi. How you have handled this matter, Toxophile, I may not well tell you myself now; but, for your gentleness and good-will towards learning and shooting, I will be content to show you any pleasure whensoever you will; and now the sun is down, therefore, if it please you, we will go home and drink in my chamber, and there I will tell you plainly what I think of this communication, and also what day we will appoint, at your request, for the other matter to meet here again.

* The instruments of shooting are *external*. * Those who write of things well-known, seldom extend their care to time in which they may be known less. This account of the *bracer* is somewhat obscure. It seems to have been a kind of close sleeve laced upon the left arm. * The note which contains the former editor's suggestion for correcting this verse is omitted. If he had looked at the first three editions, he would have seen that the word *quoth* had been left out in two places. † *Thermes*, or *tharms*, are guts. * *Tillering* is a word of art which I do not understand. * *Pith* is strength, sprightliness, vigour, power of action. * There is no mention of wooden cases before, therefore

it should perhaps be *wool cases*, unless something be left out by the printer. * The 1st edition has *ware*, the 2nd and the 3rd read *bestowe*. † Boyle somewhere mentions a Pole, who related that the cold of his country's winters broke his bow. * *Seasoned for casting*, that is, well seasoned to hinder it from warping. * This account of the qualities of the ash, which is represented as having some peculiar power of swiftness, is obscure. He probably means, that ash is the wood which in a quantity proper for an arrow, has weight enough to strike hard, and lightness enough to fly far. * *Compass heavy* seems to signify *proportionately heavy*. * *Leath* is limber, flexible, easily giving way. Milton calls it *lithe*. * If it be true, as I believe it is, that a shaft turns round in flying, it is not true that triangular shafts are good for piercing, as has been said by the author, nor that Commodus could intercept the neck of a bird between the two points of a half-moon. * *Profit and last*, convenience and duration. * This alludes to the actions of the Romish priest in public benedictions. This passage may explain a very obscure phrase in Spenser, who calls waving the sword in circles, blessing the sword. * To *fear* is to *terrify*. * *The down wind*, &c. This passage I do not fully understand.

NOTES ON THE GLOSSARY OF OLD WORDS

IN THE TOXOPHILUS

Abroach: prepared

Afore: for or before

Afrike: Africa, 79 not 80

Agglets = aglets: the metal tag of a lace

A-good: to improve

Axed: asked

Barbitons: a kind of lyre or. lute

Beched = bitched

Bobtails: arrows tapering evenly from the pile to the nock

Bole: the trunk of a tree, 108 not 100

Bolt out: to find out

Brant: steep; even brant: straight up, 79 not 70

Bray = brae: a hill-side

Chapiter: chapter

Circes: Circe, 47 not 48

Clamparde: put together hastily

Couling: shaping

Fletcher: an arrow maker

Foumards: polecats

Galiards = galliards: the music to a lively dance

Gere: airing of feelings

Girds: sudden movements

Guiles: stratagem

Hath: has

Herden: a coarse fabric made from the hards (coarse part) of
  flax or hemp

His [*for* its] own nature: 128 not 121

Hose: well-fitting

Housen: houses

Inde: India

Knoweth: knows

Leath: ⎫
Leathie weak: ⎬ flexible

Leese: lose

Leful: lawful

Lesings: lies or losses

Letted: let

Lets: hindrances

Lewdly: unlearnedly

Lipe: sudden movement

Lug: heavy and clumsy

Mastres: mistress, 31 not

45 Maul: a wooden club Maysters: masters, 87 not
71

Methink: I think

Minikin: a thin string of gut used *for* the treble string of a
lute or viol

Miscontent: discontent

Mo and Moo: many, more, 97 not 59 or 79

Morispikes = morris pikes: pikes of moorish origin, 57 not
58

Much-what: almost

Mystres see Maysters

Naughty Knife: poor quality, inferior

Nock: notch (the later way of spelling 'nock') in the tips of
the bow for the bowstring

Nocking: the act of placing the slot (nock) at the end of the
arrow onto the bowstring

Outshoot: shoot past

Overthwart: indirect

Pactyas fault: imperfection

Pavanes: slow and stately dances

Perfecter: one who does things thoroughly

Piking: trimming

Pinks: sailing ships with very narrow sterns

Port: retinue Prick-song: music sung from notes 'pricked' or
written down

Pricks: the place (any chosen spot) where the marks (target faces) are placed; butts and pricks: butts are mounds on which the marks (target faces) are placed

Quaisy: delicate, fastidious

Raught: reached

Resh: rush

Rif raff: the worthless or disreputable element of the poplace

Saith wise men: say wise men

Sallow tree: willow tree

Sambukes: triangular stringed instruments with a very sharp, shrill tone

Scout watch: the action of keeping watch and guard

Sere: individual; archer, 134 not 184

Sheering: shearing

Snudge: miser

Spence: expense

Spill: kill

Squirter and Dribber: one who shoots jerkily with a bow, 85 not 87

Stele: shaft, an arrow without feathers and head/pile

Stoore: stiff

Stour: battle

Studding or scudding: swiftly flying

Tillerings: altering a bow by scraping the wooden stave to shape it and to reduce the weight or poundage of the bow. A tiller is a gadget made of a straight piece of wood

with a notch at the end and notches on the top, in which
a bow is placed and drawn to see how it bends

Trow: believe

Unleful: unlawful

Unwares: unawares

Wap: the turn of the bowstring wrapped round the nock of
a bow

Wem: blemish

Whiles: until

Will can: well can

Wind-shake: a flaw or crack in timber due to the strain
caused by the wind

Wise and good: wise and quick-tempered

ADDITIONAL ARCHERY TERMINOLOGY

IN THE TOXOPHILUS

Bracer: a guard (Toxophilus' would have been of leather) worn on the bow-arm to protect the arm from accidental blows by the string, 99, 100, 101, 104, 105

Breasted (or chested) arrow: an arrow thickest around 6" (15.2 cm) from the nock, 120

Cast up grass: grass thrown up into the air to determine which way the wind is blowing, 93

Compass, to shoot; (or round compass): to shoot the arrow in a curved or parabolic line, 93, 99, 109, 127, 148, 155, 158, 159

Dead shaft: heavy dull arrow, 124

Down wind: the wind blowing directly from the archer to the mark (target) ie shooting with the wind, 153

Flight (arrow): an arrow designed to obtain the longest distance possible, 124

Keeping a length: to shoot the exact distance, 87, 132, 133, 146, 155, 158, 159, 162

Mark: the object (target face) shot at eg a card or a piece of white stiff paper held in place by a wooden peg or pin in the centre of it (hence the word 'pin-hole' for an arrow